# YOUR JEWELS ARE IN YOUR JOURNEY

## *Life Lessons to Lead You to Your Optimal Self*

# ELIJAH LEWIS

www.lfbookpublishing.com

**Your Jewels Are in Your Journey:**
Life Lessons to Lead You to Your Optimal Self



Summary: Your Jewels Are in Your Journey is a motivational book that delivers strategies to optimize life outcomes.

ISBN: 979-8-9882743-9-1

# TABLE OF CONTENTS

# DEDICATION

First and foremost, I would like to dedicate this work to my loved ones who have made their transition to become ancestors. I appreciate all the jewels you all gave me while you all were here on this Earth. Please know that your knowledge and wisdom has not fallen, and do not fall on deaf ears.

Next, I would like to dedicate my work to my parents, Russell and Kwajelyn Lewis, who I also appreciate for their knowledge and wisdom in my life. More importantly, thanks for always being there on my journey and being my two most important jewels as well! To my family and friends: thanks for being in my life and know this work is dedicated to you, too. I am nothing without you all, and I do not take that for granted. Finally, this work is dedicated to anyone who needs a helping hand in life. I hope this book inspires you as you travel on your journey of life moving forward.

# PREFACE

This book was written to give you the tools to be your optimal self. I wanted to use this book as a source of inspiration for others by not only giving you the life lessons that mean the most to me but also by providing you with my own experiences you can learn from as you read this book. However, I did not want this to be your typical self-help book. See, I wanted to make you feel as though you and I are having a conversation with each other, as opposed to me having a conversation with you and making it seem as though I'm talking down to you. Think of it as if we are sitting down at a table in a nice restaurant, and we're talking about the journey of life and the lessons it has to offer. There's no better feeling than knowing you can help others be the best they can be. With that said, I hope you enjoy the journey you're about to embark on as you read this book!

# CHAPTER 1

# NEVER TAKE LIFE FOR GRANTED

There are so many lessons that life can teach you. Honestly, I do not think it would be possible to put them all in a book. However, I believe these ten chapters I am providing to you are very important to take on your journey. Now, these are the lessons or jewels I have learned in my journey in life and, in some cases, am still learning. You may have more than ten and that's awesome, but at the same time I don't want to overwhelm you. So, let's start with the first important jewel to take on your journey, which is: never take life for granted.

I am sure you have heard that statement before, and to be honest, it is the truth because it is the foundation for all the other jewels you will learn in your journey. Think about it: how can you talk about life lessons and not talk about life itself? It's almost like talking about a bank but not talking about money. Doesn't make any sense, right? However, when you do not take life for granted, your perspective on life changes, you start making smarter decisions, and I think it makes you better as a person because you cannot do anything without life itself.

## Every Day is a Blessing to Live

Now, I am not a religious person, although like most people I did grow up practicing religion, and I'll touch on that a little later in the book.

But as a spiritual person, I know every day is a blessing to live. I am not trying to lead anyone on a particular path as far as your beliefs are concerned because ultimately that is your decision because it's your life. But like I said, I thank the Most High or what term you have for the deity you serve for blessing me to live another day. When we talk about not taking life for granted, we have to realize tomorrow is not promised and not everyone has the same blessing to wake up to see the next morning. Now that is unfortunate, but at the same time death, ironically, is a part of life. Of course, my fellow '90s kids know as we were taught as children when we watched "The Lion King" with the circle of life. Speaking of "The Lion King," Mufusa said it best to Simba:**"Everything you see exists together in a delicate balance, as king you need to understand that balance and respect all the creatures from the crawling ant to the leaping antelope."** He also went on to say, **"When we die, our bodies become the grass and the antelope eat the grass, and so we are connected in the great circle of life."** Not to say that's true since this is a Disney movie we're talking about, but the wisdom behind it shows life cannot be taken for granted, so much so to the point where even animals can grasp this concept.

When you think about it, without grass, certain animals cannot live. The same applies to us when it comes to food, shelter, clothes, etc. In life, sometimes we get so caught up in what we do not have that we forget what we do have. You may not have the newest car or biggest house, and there is nothing wrong with having top of the line things. But ask yourself: do you have food, water, shelter, and good health? Never take life for granted as far as what you possess because there are people who may not be as fortunate as you, or who would love to have what you have. Also, remember the older you get to always be thankful. Every birthday you get to celebrate is a reminder you should never take life for granted. I know we all like to talk about how we're getting old as we age, but when you think about it, there are a lot of people who do not make it to the age you currently are. For example, I'm twenty-five, soon to be twenty-six years old at the time of writing, and it saddens me when I hear people who are my age or close to my age pass away. When you're young, death is not something you think about, but unfortunately it happens, The lesson is to be thankful you have made it on another year on this Earth and remember it's not necessarily that you're getting older; it means you're getting better. That leads me to my next point.

## Everyday is an Opportunity to Get Better

As you get older, you should be getting better. The ultimate goal in life should be progression, not perfection, because we are humans and will make mistakes. I'll expound on that in the next chapter. The main point is that every day when we wake up, we should strive to be better than we were yesterday. The beauty about life is we have the ability to get better, and we do not have to stay in one place our entire lives, both figuratively and literally. You get better by taking it one day at a time; remember a little progress is better than no progress at all.

If you take life for granted, you never see the value of getting better. In fact, you will find yourself stuck in the same place you have been. An example of this might be if you are trying to lose weight, you know you're going to have to exercise and clean up your diet. It might not be a good idea to say that you're immediately going to run three miles a day. You may have to just try going for a walk for fifteen to thirty minutes and slowly build from there until you know you could handle three miles. When it comes to your diet, you are going to have to learn to substitute sweets for fruits or vegetables if you like to snack, as opposed to something like fried chicken or pizza for dinner. I'm not a doctor or personal trainer, but I'm sure if you take the proper steps to better yourself in your weight, I'm sure you will get to the weight you want. Just take it one day at a time.

Now, I believe if you have a take life for granted mindset, you won't get to the weight you want, and you will only be making your health worse. So, it's important to realize every day is an opportunity to get better as long as you realize not to take life for granted. An example of taking the opportunity to get better for me was the summer of 2013 when I went to the Y (YMCA) to swim. I was on the swim team the previous year, but I was not as good as I thought I should be. This was a good opportunity to practice the various swim styles and get ready for the next swim season. I remember when my high school gave out awards for athletics, I won "Most Improved Swimmer." In fact, I remember one of my coaches saying jokingly, but probably being very serious, that "last season Elijah couldn't swim a lap" as he gave me the award, but I sure he saw the change that past season. In fact, practicing at the Y is what helped me participate at a Swim-A-Thon where I swam multiple laps. Had I not practiced at the Y, I know I would not have gotten better at swimming, and I probably would not get the award for "Most Improved Swimmer." But because I realized that every day is an opportunity to get better, I made the most of it to the point where I'm pretty confident when it comes to swimming. In fact, being on the swim team was actually the inspiration that made me want to be a lifeguard for four years. Now I'm not the best swimmer ever or the next Michael Phelps, but your boy can get around a pool. With that I say, remember to strive to get better every day and watch what can happen.

## You Don't Know When It's Your Last Day on Earth

The interesting thing about life is we never know when it's our last day to be alive. It's interesting how we know when we were born, but we do not know when we are going to experience death. Honestly, I think that is a good thing in the sense it does make us have to appreciate life even more. If we knew the exact moment our lives would end, we probably would not appreciate life the way we do or should. We would not appreciate the time we spend with family or friends, vacations, proms, graduations, weddings, or any important milestones we experience if we knew when our end was going to be. Again, this is just another reason why we must value the jewel of never taking life for granted. In fact, it is great to be thankful you have not experienced your last day on Earth yet because you would not have been able to achieve the accomplishments of your life or to continue to go after your goals and dreams that you still have yet to accomplish.

When you reflect on your life, I am sure there are moments where you might have thought it was going to be or might have been your last day on Earth, whether it was an illness, a car accident, growing up in a bad neighborhood, or whatever your unique situation. But be thankful you made it through because that is what is most important. Two examples for me are experiencing pneumonia twice and being inside a car hit by a bus. The first time I experienced pneumonia was when I was two, so I do not have any memories of it, thank God, but I definitely remember the second time. In March 2009, I'll never forget I was shoveling the snow and when I finished, I went back in the house. I was complaining about being so cold and tired that I just laid on the couch, and I could not get up to save my life. As the week went on, I got sicker and sicker. I remember not being able to eat anything and really being in a miserable state. Once my parents took me to the doctor, I was told I actually had double pneumonia. I guess pneumonia wanted to come back with a vengeance on me this time.

The other example is when I was in a car was hit by a bus in guess what year…2009. Looking back, 2009 was a very interesting year for me in the fact my life pretty much flashed before my eyes twice that year. That's something I couldn't understand at twelve years old. In October 2009, my mom and I were heading to the church we used to be a part of another sister and her daughter who were members of the church as well. When we got to church, the car was parked on the side of the street, so we were ready to get out. My mom had already gotten out and we were going to do the same. Well as I am getting ready to get out of the car, I noticed an MTA bus (that's the bus company in Baltimore) coming closer to the door I am getting ready to get out of. Now, I'm thinking the bus is going to continue to turn the corner and go up the street, only to find out it was coming straight at me. I remember getting ready to close the door and bracing for the impact. Believe me, it was a hard impact, but thankfully I was not hurt. However, I'm glad something in my spirit told me not to get out of the car because this could have gone a totally different way. What I do remember was that my mom was in a total state of panic after the accident because she had gotten out of the car and was fortunate to have only suffered a few bumps and bruises. But I remember her panic of whether or not I was okay because the bus had hit the door area where I was sitting. To be honest, this might have been the first time I can remember ever seeing her in a state of panic. In fact, I can remember shedding a few tears for two reasons. The first reason was tears of joy that I was okay, and the second reason was I felt for her panicking about whether or not her only child was okay. The good news was everyone was okay in the accident, but this definitely did leave me in a state of shock.

Thankfully, neither one of these experiences were my last days on Earth. If anything, they made me appreciate life even more and be thankful for the time that I still have. Now speaking of time, I saw a picture on Facebook that said "The biggest mistake we have in life is thinking we have time" with a picture of Kobe Bryant. Honestly, that does hit you differently especially when you realize that we've lost a legend like Kobe. I'll never forget where I was on January 26, 2020 when I heard the heartbreaking news that Kobe had passed away. I was ironing clothes for the week, and I saw some posts about Kobe's death on social media, but there is always a question of whether what you're hearing is real. I believe my mom told me to turn on the news, and there it was: breaking news, Kobe Bryant had died at the age of forty-one in a helicopter crash.

The biggest mistake we make is we sometimes think our favorite celebrities are immortal and death is something they will never experience. I think that's why the world stops when we lose a huge public figure like Kobe because we forget celebrities are still human. Now that doesn't mean they still won't live on through their craft. As the late Lisa "Left Eye" Lopes once said, **"Energy never dies. It just transforms."** So I'm sure there are many NBA players who still feel Kobe's energy when they step on the court, especially if they played with him or against him throughout his career. For me, Kobe was and will always be my favorite player; he was my generation's Michael Jordan. Then again, he did model his game after Michael, so it makes sense. But when he did pass away, it honestly felt like a piece of my childhood had passed away as well. Growing up like most kids, I can remember shooting a paper ball in a trash can yelling "Kobe," playing NBA 2K always as the Lakers, mainly cause I'm a diehard Lakers fan, and even having a Kobe 24 Lakers jersey and a Lakers hat with the Kobe 24 on the side (all I need now is a Lakers Kobe #8 jersey, and I'll be straight). Of course, my two favorite Kobe memories are him and the Lakers beating the Celtics in the 2010 NBA Finals and his final game when he scored 60 points on the Jazz. I sure wish I could remember watching him score 81 on the Raptors in 2006, but I'll take the 60 in 2016. Man, it sure is weird having a world of basketball with no Kobe Bryant, and it's even sadder that we were starting to watch him pass down his love and passion for the game of basketball to his daughter Gianna at the time of their deaths.

The point in all of this is to say we all think we have time to procrastinate when the reality is we really don't. When we look at all the things Kobe accomplished, it is mainly because he never procrastinated. The man worked hard to be the best NBA player in the game and ultimately, in my opinion, in the conversation of the top ten greatest players of all time. In fact, it's part of the reason the Mamba Mentality has become so iconic because he gave it all he had and left nothing in the tank. We don't know when our last day on Earth is going to be, and we don't know how much time we are going to have left, so it's important you give it your all in whatever passion you have whether it's teaching, cooking, singing, or (like Kobe) basketball. I guess we all need to have the Mamba Mentality in life because when it's all said and done you want to look back and say I gave it my all. Michael Jordan said it best at Kobe and Gianna's memorial service, "**No one knows how much time we have. That's why we must live in the moment, we must endure the moment. We must reach and see and spend as time as we can with our families and friends and the people that we absolutely love. To live in the moment means to enjoy each and every one that we come in contact with.**" So you may not know when your last day on Earth is, but as long as you're alive, give it your all and take the opportunity to enjoy every moment you can with your loved ones and friends because that's the thing: you never know when it will be your turn to say goodbye. I'll end this section with a quote from Redd Foxx. He said, "**You folks who don't smoke, I want to let you know that you gone die from something else. But ya gone die, nobody ever stayed here. If they did, where's Abraham Lincoln** tonight? I'll tell you, he's somewhere in a long coffin with that tall f**king hat on."

## Life is What You Make It

When it comes to not taking life for granted, I think it's important to analyze your perspective on life itself. How you view and perceive life determines how you're going to make your version of life. If you have a positive view on life, chances are life might be positive to you. If you have a negative view on life, chances are life might be negative. Now I can't guarantee you anything because you're still going to go through challenges and obstacles because that's part of life, but even your perspective of life can determine whether or not you overcome those challenges and obstacles. The Bible does say that "as a man thinketh so is he." So it is all about your attitude because with the right attitude, you certainly won't take life for granted. I just hope the life you make is positive and you make the most of it.

## My Final Conservation with My Grandfather

If there is one person who I can truly give the credit for teaching me to never take life for granted, it would be my grandfather. I'll never forget the last conversation I had with him before he made his transition to become an ancestor. The main point of the conversation from what I can remember was about reflecting on life. What I remember the most from the conversation was that when it came to life, he told me that he was satisfied. Despite the fact he had been dealing with health challenges, I was happy for him that he felt that way. To be honest, I am of the firm belief our elders know they are going to make their transition soon, and they want to take their final opportunity to say goodbye. I did not know it at the time, but when I look back on it, I feel like that was his way of saying goodbye to me. Of course, I did say goodbye to him when I left his house later that evening, but to me that conversation always stood out to me. In fact, I would probably say it was my favorite memory of the twenty years I got to know him.

A few weeks later on May 2, 2017, my grandfather made his transition at the age of eighty-nine. To prove my point about our elders knowing that it's their time to go, I remember my step-grandmother telling me he had said that he had reached his measured time. After his death, our last conservation really stuck with me.

To me, I think his death sunk in when I went to his house after his passing and there was no one sitting in his chair. If anyone in my family knows, this was like his throne. I just could never bring myself to sit in it, especially after his passing. One of the things my grandfather had also talked about was making it to my graduation at Tuskegee. I was told by some of my family he would say, "If I can just make it to Elijah's graduation." I always appreciated the love and support he gave me. In our last conversation, we talked about my graduation, and he said, "If I can get out of bed and put a hat on my head, I'll be there." Well he was there in spirit and that is what inspired me to have someone design my Tuskegee grad cap as a tribute to all of my family members who could not be there to celebrate with me.

If anything, my grandfather inspired me to want to look at my past with satisfaction. When I think of my grandfather, I think of a person who didn't take life for granted, raised his family, and achieved what he wanted to do to ensure he lived his life to the fullest. My ultimate goal would be to sit down with my grandson or granddaughter and express to him or her how satisfied I have been with my life when I get to be my grandfather's age. I think that is a desire that we all have, to know we did everything we wanted in life and are satisfied because when you get to the end of life and you're not satisfied, then you might have to ask what was the purpose of living. By the way, for those of you who still are blessed to have your grandparents in your life, do not forget to check on them, you never know what experiences you will have with them that you'll carry for the rest of your life.

# Notes and Insights

# CHAPTER 2

# You Can Learn from Your Mistakes

As I stated previously, life is about progression, not perfection. We're human, and that is why the phrase "nobody is perfect" is popular. But if you're going to progress through life, you're going to have to learn from your mistakes.

## Learning from Your Mistakes Makes You Better

When you think about where you are today and the person you have become, I'm sure you made a lot of mistakes along the way, and that's okay. What is important is how you respond to them moving forward. It is also important to know the difference between a mistake and a decision. Paulo Coelho said that **"a mistake repeated more than once is not a mistake anymore. It is a decision."** So, if you are not learning from your mistakes, you're not getting better. You're actually making the decision to remain where you are, and that is not progression. That's actually hesitation.

A great example of learning from your mistakes to become better is in the world of sports. For those of you who play or have played sports know that you win some and you lose some. When you see a team lose a game, it is usually because multiple mistakes were made such as penalties, turnovers, and missed opportunities. However, what separates the great from the average is they learn from their mistakes. They realize their weaknesses and ensure they learn from them and get better for the next game. That's the reason they practice and watch film because practice and studying make you better. The teams that are average or flat-out trash don't do that and keep making the same mistakes. The definition of insanity is doing the same thing over and over and expecting a different result.

Another example would be in the world of academics when it comes to taking a test. We all have taken a test in school in which we did not study like we should and did not pass. Then again, every now and then, we got lucky. But the lesson here usually is to not wait until the last minute to start studying. Join a study group or maybe attend your professor's office hours to better understand the subject. The bottom line is mistakes are teaching tools to allow you to better yourself, and they are universal in any area to achieve success.

## It's Okay to Admit You're Wrong

Part of learning from your mistakes is to know when you are wrong and be comfortable admitting you are wrong. It's like the old saying goes, **"The first step to solving a problem is to admit you have one in the first place."** As painful as it is for some people, you will never be right all the time. Admitting you're wrong is the first step to growth and becoming better. People who always think they are right all the time never grow or become better. In fact, that is a narcissistic attitude. The main characteristic of a narcissist is that they can never admit any wrongdoing, and it is always someone else's fault. Now I hope that's not you because if it is, people are going to dislike you for it. Most people who are not narcissists do not have much respect for narcissistic people.

An example of me having to admit that I was wrong was when I was in middle school, and I had gotten into a fight with another student. What started the fight was me saying something about the student's mom, which looking back at the situation, I am definitely not proud of. Now I am not saying I am for violence, but I understand why he did it. As men, there are certain things we are not going to let you be disrespectful about and get away with, and that includes a man's mom, girlfriend or wife, grandmother, or pretty much any woman he has a high level of respect for since as men it is our nature to protect and provide. Now if you do not believe me, look at what happened at the 2022 Oscars between Will Smith and Chris Rock. Of course, I am a fan of both of them like many people are as both men are talented in their craft. I am not here to say who was right or wrong between the two, but it is an example of what happens when a man says something about a woman that a man has respect for; and in feeling disrespected, the other man slapped him. Going back to my situation, I guess you can say I felt like Chris Rock, but the only difference was I did not say what I said in a joking kind of way. Of course, I didn't say, "Oh wow, wow!" either.

In the end, it boiled down to the phrase, **"If you don't have anything nice to say, don't say it all."** To be honest, it is one of the moments of my life that I regret. I am not ashamed to admit he did win the fight, but I did learn my lesson for sure. Now I know what Proverbs 15:1 was referring to when it says, **"A soft answer turneth away wrath: but grievous words stir up anger."** and when Proverbs 17:28 says, **"Even a fool, when he holdeth his peace, is counted wise: and he that shutteth his lips is esteemed a man of understanding."** If the brother who punched me for what I said is reading this see this, then I personally want to apologize to you and your mother because that was a very foolish action on my part, and I am man enough to admit my mistakes.

With that said, never be afraid to admit you are wrong because that is how you learn and get better. You just have to take the L, dust yourself off, and be willing to improve. Also, let's learn to respect each other because there is nothing great about seeing two people fight, especially over something that could have been avoided in the first place.

## You Don't Know It All Like You Think You Do

To learn from your mistakes, you are going to have to realize you do not know everything like you think you do. Then again, who does? As human beings we are not all knowing, so we are going to have to obtain knowledge as we go about life. There's a quote in my parents' home that says, **"At no point is the spiritual journey finished. At no point does anyone know all there is to know. Knowledge is infinite."** Obtaining knowledge allows you to not only become better in your actions or provide more intelligence but also gives you the blueprint of how not to make the same mistake twice. One of my favorite people who I like to listen to is Dr. Ray Hagins, who is a psychologist, educator, and international chief elder and spiritual leader of the Afrikan Village and Cultural Center. Before Dr. Hagins starts off his lectures, he asks his audience to take their fingers and make a circle as he says these words, **"The space inside this circle represents my realm of knowledge. All that I think I know about whatever I think I know is depicted right here within this circle! I must keep in mind that there is more to know than what is within the circumference of my awareness!"** The main point to realize from this is to understand you may know a lot of information, but you do not know all the information there is to know.

Knowledge is power, but if you truly knew it all, then why would you need to go to school or read books, conduct research, or have teachers? People might say there is power in the more you know, which I believe is true, but I would say there is more power in the more you learn. Without learning, there is no knowing. An example of me realizing you do not know it all like you think you do was when my father had asked me what I planned to do if I did not go to college. Now the backstory behind this was that I was placed on academic probation by my high school, Baltimore Polytechnic Institute. I received a letter from Poly putting me on academic probation during my sophomore year because I was failing some classes, which I will explain why a little later in this book. Now if anyone who has graduated Poly knows that sophomore year can be hard as hell. Two math classes on top of all the other classes and work you are getting is not easy. In fact, my sophomore year at Poly was my worst school year ever, not just in high school, but any school year period. Now when I gave my father the letter from Poly stating that I was on academic probation, he asked when I had realized I was failing, and he was not calm about either. I felt that the times my father yelled at me, he yelled so loud I am sure people in California could hear him. Maybe he was the reason California has so many earthquakes. Then again, my father is a Gemini, so that might explain it because Geminis have the side you want to see and the side you don't want to see. But I know he was not doing it from a place of malice but from a place of concern.

My response to my dad's question was I learned I was failing when I got the letter. I did not say this to him, but in my mind, I was thinking that I did not want him to be mad at me because I had high self-esteem." Parents, let me be real for a second when I say that nine out of ten times, most children are not going to admit to you that they're failing; most likely they don't want to deal with how you will react. I am sure some of you all have been there when you were students yourselves. So, when he had asked what I planned to do if I did not attend college, I said I did not know, and I would probably get a job at Walmart. To be honest,

I never really thought of that, but in the moment, I was trying to give him an answer to his question and act like I had a plan laid out for the future. He asked how much money do you plan to make a year, and I said $10,000. His response in the most brutally honest way was, 'Yeah… in 1970." So that pretty much crushed my plan. Cut me some slack though because in my teenage mind $10,000 a year was definitely a lot of money. Hey, it was $10,000 more dollars than I had at the time! My response was that I was not trying to be rich and that I wanted a regular job. Little did I know I was giving my version of the "Theo speech" from "The Cosby Show."

If you ever saw the pilot episode of "The Cosby Show", you will remember the scene where Theo and Dr. Huxtable are discussing his poor grades, and Theo informs his father that he is not going to college. He states that he wants to "**get a job like regular people**" and "**work at a gas station, drive a bus, something like that.**" In his opinion, "**you don't need good grades to be regular people.**" Of course, we get to the famous scene where Dr. Huxtable uses Monopoly money to demonstrate why his plan won't work as well as he thinks it does. What Theo failed to recognize is he had got to account for necessities such as food, clothing, a vehicle, and shelter, not to mention taxes. The icing on the cake is when he asks Theo if he plans to have a girlfriend, and he replies "for sure". Then his father takes his last $200 in Monopoly money and sarcastically says, "**regular people.**" After seeing that episode so many times, I see myself in Theo and see why he felt like that. Ironically, someone told me that I reminded them of Theo when I got to Tuskegee.

The biggest lesson I have learned is you may have a plan, but you may not know all the details of your plan that you need to know. It's one of those experiences where as a teenager you think you reached the age where you believe you know more than your parents, but the reality is you really don't know what you are talking about. If anything, this experience with my father made me realize I needed to do better and set higher expectations for myself than I actually had. Now, this is not me trying to look down at people who work at Walmart or have so-called regular jobs because I respect anyone who is trying to make an honest living, but sometimes you have people who see something in you that you may not see in yourself, and they can warn you if they see what you think you know could potentially backfire on you. Finally, this experience leads me to my next point which is…

## Humility Is Greater Than Your Ego

Honestly, I did not know I was failing when I got my high academic probation letter, but my ego wouldn't allow me to realize it, mainly because I had never done poorly in school before. So when you are a former straight-A student in middle school, and you have now gone to being on academic probation, it becomes a shock that you may not be willing to accept right away. That's when your ego comes in to make it seem that there is nothing wrong with what you're doing even though you know there is. As much as we hate to see our ego get hurt, the harsh reality is there are moments where it is going to happen, and we are going to have to be humbled.

As long as you are controlled by your ego, you don't allow yourself to learn from your mistakes, because your ego will always say you are right and everyone else is wrong. Now humility does not mean you are weak; it just means you are willing to learn and become better without having the need to be full of yourself. Booker T. Washington said it best when he said, **"Egotism is the anesthetic that dulls the pain of stupidity."** The way I understand that is the ego is the drug a person can use to justify their bad decision making. It can be used as an escape from their bad decision making as well. A person with a lot of ego has a hard time with humility because they believe they are always above any wrongdoing. But as long as you are human, there are moments where you are going to do something wrong, so you can't let your ego control you. You have to learn and realize that day by day the goal is to figure out how to be better than you were yesterday. As Kendrick Lamar said on his song, "HUMBLE", **"sit down, be humble,"** or as he recently said on his latest album, 'Mr. Morale and the Big Steppers" with the song, "Count Me Out", **"But a mask won't hide who you are inside, Look around, the realities carved in the lies, Wipe my ego, dodge my pride (and I'm trippin' and fallin'), Look myself in the mirror."** See your ego is like a mask that does not allow you to be the real you or the optimal version of you. It really is a way to cover up any insecurities or flaws you have, but it does not allow you to change or correct those insecurities or flaws. That leads to hesitation in your growth. But as Kendrick said, you are going to have to wipe your ego, dodge your pride, and look at yourself in the mirror because once you do that, you are on the first step to being your optimal self.

The moment I realized humility is better than ego is when I was involved in a car accident in 2021 due to me falling asleep at the wheel. Whenever I do long-distance driving, my parents always ask if I am well rested. This is usually the case when I go back and forth from Waldorf to Baltimore every other weekend, since I work in Indian Head, MD as an engineer with NAVSEA. I would always say that I was well rested. They would offer me some things to keep me awake whether it was an energy drink or energy pills. But to be honest, I felt like I never needed those things to keep me awake and that I knew when my body had reached its limit. Sometimes, I would pull over and take a nap if I had to, but I felt that was all I needed. Well, my luck had run out on Friday, August

13, 2021 when I accidentally rear ended a family's SUV by falling asleep at the wheel. Then again, they do say bad things happen on Friday the 13th. While I was driving from Waldorf to Baltimore, I did feel myself getting tired, and my plan was to pull over to get some rest, but I nodded off for a second, and when I came to, I could not slow my car down enough to avoid hitting the SUV in front of me.

First and foremost, everyone was okay in the accident and walked away unscathed, but this did humble me tremendously because my parents had proved their point that before I do any long-distance traveling, I needed to be well rested or have something that will keep me awake because this situation was far worse than it could have been. My irresponsible actions could have hurt myself or the family I hit or even worse. Plus, I had to get a brand-new car because my car was totaled and not worth the full repair since it was an older model, so it took a toll on me mentally, physically, and especially financially. I should have listened to my parents instead of my ego. However, I believe that accident made me a better driver because now I emphasize getting as much rest as possible or having something to keep me awake when driving for a long period of time. I reflect on the fact that my parents were not being overbearing, but they wanted me to be as safe as possible on the road. But the only reason I could get to this point was being humble and casting my ego to the side because if you are not careful your ego can hurt you…literally.

## It's Okay to Change and Change is Good

We have spent a lot of time focusing on learning from mistakes we make in life, but we have yet to highlight the most important aspect which is change. Change is that moment a person decides to do something different to improve a situation or outcome. Change is a good thing because it keeps us from being stagnant in our development as we go through life.

Think about it, how would life be if people did not change? If people did not change, we would never reach our full potential. An example of a person who changed and was able to obtain their full potential is Malcolm X.

If you have ever read "The Autobiography of Malcolm X," you learned how Malcolm became one of the greatest leaders in the history of the world. You have a man who wanted to be a lawyer but was discouraged from doing so because his teacher thought he needed to be more realistic than that. In fact, due to the overt racism of the day, the teacher said that he could not be a lawyer and a ni**er at the same time. Think about how painful it would be for your teacher to tell you that being a lawyer is "no realistic expectation for a ni**er." He drops out of school at fourteen years old and goes down a path of crime to the point he ends up in prison.

However, while in prison, we see how he becomes influenced to read and eventually converted to the Nation of Islam to become one of the greatest freedom fighters of the black community. Now, I am not saying you need to convert to a religious group to obtain change, but Malcolm's story is a perfect demonstration that it is not how you start; it is how you finish. Had he not realized the importance of change in his life, we may not know Malcolm X the way we do today.

Although his life was cut short at thirty-nine years old, the man accomplished more in his life than most people do in their entire lifetime mainly through his leadership, determination, and commitment to serving his people. All this happened because he made the decision to change. One of Malcolm's greatest quotes is **"Education is the passport to the future, for tomorrow belongs to those who prepare for it today."**

When you make the decision to make a change, you will be surprised at what you can achieve. Ultimately, change starts with your mindset. If you know you need to change, but you refuse, you will not achieve much. Again, insanity is doing the same thing repeadedly and expecting different results, so do not be afraid to change. Also, it is important to realize anyone can change for the better and not to let your past hold you back from changing. Again, you're going to make mistakes, but it is how you respond to those mistakes that counts. As Donnie McClurkin said on his song "We Fall Down," " **We fall down, but we get up. For a saint is just a sinner who fell down, but we couldn't stay there, and got up."** Pay attention to the key lyric when he says, **"but we couldn't stay there."** That's the beauty and the power or change; you have the ability to come back from your mistakes. You do not have to feel stuck. Above all else, you have the ability to make things right. Most people like to see someone power of change for the better because it can be a source of inspiration in their own life. Sometimes the best teaching tool is to learn from others' experiences.

In fact, in the book "How To Win Friends & Influence People" by Dale Carnegie, one of the key lessons is to "**talk about your own mistakes first**" and to "**talk about your own mistakes before criticizing the other person.**" So, it is important you make the change within yourself before you expect others to do the same. The Bible talks about how you cannot pull the mote out of your brother's eye until you cast the beam that's in your eye. Remember when it comes to change, never let people gaslight you for making a change for the better because average people do not like people who make a change. They would much rather everyone remain the same even if it is to their detriment.

Finally, I will end this chapter about learning from your mistakes and the power of change with one more scene from "The Lion King" in which Rafiki meets Simba after he speaks with his father in the clouds to inform him he has to take his place as king back at Pride Rock. Rafiki starts off by saying, "What was that? The weather, very peculiar, don't you think?" To which Simba replies, "Looks like the winds are changing." Rafiki's response, "**Ah, change is good.**" Simba responds with, "**Yeah, but it's not easy. I know what I have to do, but going back means I'll have to change my past. I've been running from it for so long.**" Rafiki takes his stick and smacks him on the head with it, to which Simba asks him, "What was that for?" Rafiki says, "**It doesn't matter, it's in the past.**" Now this is an interesting and, to be honest, painful way to teach someone a lesson, but here is the key point. Simba says, "Yeah, but it still hurts." Rafiki's response is that "**Oh yes, the past can hurt, but the way I see it you can either run from it or learn from it.**" He tries to hit him a second time, but he ducks and he eventually heads back to Pride Rock to take his place as king.

The biggest lesson from this scene is that you have two options when dealing with your past: running from it or learning from it. You can try to run from your past like we all have tried to do at some point in our lives, but the reality is it will continue to follow you wherever you go. The only option you have is to learn from it and become better. Change to be your optimal self; that is what I want for you. Be the best version of you. Now if you still want to run from your mistakes and not learn to become better, then maybe you need someone to smack you upside the head to get the lesson in all this…figuratively, of course.

# Notes and Insights

# CHAPTER 3

# HAVE A GREAT ROLE MODEL

When Kendrick Lamar begins his song "Count Me Out" with "We may not know which way to go on this dark road," it paints a very interesting picture of how life can be without guidance because life can be a confusing road to follow if you do not have someone to look up to along the way. When you think about the journey of life, you need to think about where you are going and how you are going to get there. It is sort of how when you're driving to a place you have never been to before; you use your navigation to guide you to your destination. Well, your navigation in this sense is to have a great role model. By having a great role model, you have an individual in your corner teaching you how to be a great example to others, advising on what to do and not to do in life, and giving you the wisdom to navigate you on your journey. The biggest blessing of all is when you find that one person who can serve as a role model, you will realize that life may not seem as much of a dark road as it seems to be.

## It's Not What You Know But Who You Know

As we go throughout life, we naturally gain knowledge. While gaining a lot of knowledge, it is easy to rely on the knowledge you have gained versus realizing who gave you the knowledge. Networking with people is a huge benefit to one's success because you are gaining insight, wisdom, and mentorship from someone who can be a guide to your success. Knowing a good role model in some ways can be a bigger benefit than having a bunch of knowledge because, like I said in the previous chapter, no one knows it all. At the same time, there is no benefit in having knowledge that is not applied. With that said, who you know is critical.

An example of this is when you are in college, and you may be starting an internship or a new job. You certainly have gained a lot of knowledge in your major while at your college or university, but while having an internship or starting a new job, you may not have the experience in applying what you have learned. With that said, you may be set up with a mentor who can help propel you throughout your career and can give you the experience you need. This leads me to the next point which is…

## Experience Can Be the Best Teaching Tool

The benefit of having a great role model is you can rely on their experience whether it's positive or negative. A person can also learn from the mistakes their role model has made as well. Experience can be summarized through the African proverb: "**The youth can walk faster, but the elder knows the road.**" I view this by seeing the youth have a lot of capability and potential to travel, but it is the elderly that have the knowledge and experience to travel the road correctly, to avoid the obstacles of the road, etc. It is important to utilize the wisdom and expertise of those who came before you because that can determine how the next generation will come into play.

One reason I say experience can be the best teaching tool is that it fills in the knowledge gap someone might have in a particular subject or area of interest. Some examples might be if a tutor has experience learning algebra and the student they are tutoring has never taken an algebra class. Their experience with algebra may help that student succeed in algebra by giving them the skills they need to succeed in the class. Another example might be a coach used to winning going to a team that has been losing for a long period of time. That coach's experience from a winning culture can transform the attitude of that particular team. The coach brings confidence, leadership, and respect to that team. All of a sudden, the team was known for losing is starting to win because they listen to their coach's experience. The bottom line is a person's experience can benefit you tremendously especially when you have no prior experience of your own to go by.

## We All Have Someone We Look Up To

The reason having a great role model is an important jewel is because we all have someone in our life who we've looked up to at some point. This person could be a teacher, parent, coach, friend, or whoever you view as a role model. In my opinion, it's impossible to say you don't have a role model in your life. We all have one person in our lives who we know we wouldn't be the person who we are today without. That person gave you the wisdom, morality, and knowledge you need to get to where you are. It's important you thank that person and not take them for granted because you may not be where you are today without them. Remember, no one reaches success by themselves. It takes some help along the way and when you get to the top remember that person who helped you along the way.

## We All Have Someone Who Looks Up to Us Even If We Don't Know Who They Are

There is an old saying in life that **"what goes around, comes around."** So, the same way you had a role model growing up, there is a chance that someone might be looking at you as a role model, even if you don't know who that person is. It's important to realize people are always watching you. Another old expression is that **"you don't get a second chance to make a first expression."** That means people are watching you from the first time you meet them. People are always looking for someone to follow, especially if they lead by example. If you are someone who strives to be an upstanding citizen in society, who has morals, is ambitious, has a great work ethic, then people are going to take notice. Never belittle yourself to the point that you think no one is looking up to you. Remember, you do not need a high status to be a role model.

A lot of people can say they know a person who didn't have the highest bank account or greatest status, but they still had a positive impact on them. The bottom line is you never know who you're planting a seed for in life and who will remember and appreciate you when a person travels on their journey.

## Why Our Children Need Role Models

I'm sure we have all heard of Proverbs 22:6, which says, **"Train up a child in the way he should go: and when he is old, he will not depart from it."** When you think about it, that scripture explains the importance of children having role models. Now to reiterate, I am not trying to push any religious path on anyone, but there is great wisdom in that passage. Children are like sponges; they're going to absorb the energy around them whether it's positive or negative. Whatever you present in front of a child, that is what they are going to follow. In fact, it goes back to my last point that you never know who is watching you. Children are always watching you, whether you know it or not, which is why it's important you're setting the right example in front of them. I sure parents may wonder where their kids learn certain behaviors; a lot of times it simply comes down to what is set before them.

People often say "**that children are our future,**" and I agree. They are the ones who will receive the torch from us. That starts from the lessons we give them because we have to give them the proper guidance in order for them to succeed and to not make the same mistakes of the previous generation. After all, we should want our children to do better than we do because "**those who don't know their history are doomed to repeat it.**" If children don't thrive to build off the lessons we taught them, have we really been role models to them?

Remember "**it takes a village to raise a child.**" We can't have the attitude of not thinking it's important to teach our children because our future is doomed if we don't. Of course, we need to teach our kids how to read, write, learn math, etc. But it is also important that we teach the values of how to be productive members of society, how to respect each other, and encourage them to be their optimal self to the best of their society. Honestly, my parents did a great job of being great examples for me. I am not sure where I'd be without them. They did an excellent job of raising me and giving me morals I still carry with me in adulthood. As I have grown, one of the things my parents told me is they were told by other adults how good of a child I was. Honestly, I have to give the credit to them because they were doing their job to raise me into the man I am today, and that is what our children need today. Some of the lessons they taught me were the importance of reading, how to dress, and how to be smart with your money.

## My Role Model

As I mentioned, my parents did a tremendous job raising me. However, if I had to say who is my role model, I would have to say my father. Now this is no slight to my mother; she did an excellent job in raising me. In fact, she played a major role in my education and helped in various extracurricular activities as well, mainly the swim team and a tutoring program at Morgan State University called AMIE (Advancing Minorities' Interest in Engineering). But the reason I would say my father has always been my role model is because of the example he has set for me as far as how to be a man. Our children need both of our parents in their lives, but our sons need their fathers to teach them how to be men, and our children need both parents to teach them how to be women. As a son, that is what my father did for me.

The earliest indication that I saw from my father that made me proud to call him my role model was actually one I cannot remember because I was a year old. I was told that one morning all that was in our refrigerator was one hot dog and something to drink. Now the backstory of why this was the case was that my parents were in a financial struggle due to my mom not working because she was not teaching during the summer and my father had been unemployed in insurance for eleven years and had been working dead end jobs. To make ends meet, he was trying to get his Dry Wash business up and running while he was cleaning people's cars. Unfortunately, no one signed up to join him in business except our mechanic. But the one thing I admire about my father is that he is not a quitter. He has an excellent work ethic I believe I got from him. He knew his son had to eat that day, and one of the things he had done was he brought a fax machine to print flyers for his business. Fortunately, a customer gave him a call to get two of his cars for $150, and he was able to feed his family. One of things he told me was it felt good being able to take care of his family as a man. I can see that because no man in his right state of mind is going to feel a sense of pride in not being able to protect and provide for his family.

Even though I have no memory of all this happening, which to a degree is a good thing because I certainly would not want to see that image of our refrigerator with only a hot dog and something to drink, it makes me feel proud that my father did what he had to do to make sure I was taken care of as a child. What he did was teach his one-year-old son how to be a man without me realizing it. The lesson I take from this is that no matter how hard life gets, a man still has to take care of his responsibilities. In fact, my father told me that he hated his dry wash work. I know he told me he was washing cars in the hot sun, and he made $300. Of course, he was exhausted, but when he came home that day, I was so excited to see him that I ran and gave him a hug. I guess as a little kid, I never looked at the hardship my father was going through, but I looked up to him like any son would his father when he comes up. I guess you can say it was like looking up to a superhero for me.

As I got older, my father was a big help to my educational success as well, especially in high school. Despite him yelling at me during my academic struggles, he did a great job pushing me to be better than I was. In fact, I will never forget when my father and I were sitting in the car while I was in high school and he told me that he thought he had failed me. This was mainly due to the fact that I had not been doing academically in school or doing any extracurricular activities, which had made my chances of getting to college very dim. In his opinion, had I continued on the path that I was on, he would have seen certain members of my family not saying the most positive things about not only me but also him. I never looked at it that way, but I can now see where he was coming from because as men, we do have a lot of responsibility to be the head of the household. My father told me that in his life, a lot of people wanted to see him fail, but he was determined to not let that happen.

My father also did a great job putting me in various programs that were tremendous to my success. The two that stand out to me are the Urban Youth Racing School and the National Youth Racing School. The

Urban Youth Racing School was a great opportunity for me because I was able to learn about the world of racing, which was great because I am a huge fan of NASCAR in their Build a Dream Program. It was even cool that we even went go-kart racing as well. By the way, did I mention that while I was racing one time, I glanced at the scoreboard and saw that I was leading in practice for a second, and when I focused on the track again, I ran into the wall. Definitely keep your eyes on the road, and I did that right in front of my father, which was a funny moment between the both of us. Also, the racing was great in learning engineering and introducing me to the world of NAVSEA, which is where I work as an engineer today. One of the projects we had in their Naval Engines Program was to design a ship that could solve a world crisis, which we presented to the racing school, the employees of NAVSEA, and our families. Finally, the racing school was able to get me in contact with a fellow Tuskegee alum, Jimmy Smith, who was able to help me get a NAVSEA scholarship to attend Tuskegee University. The interesting thing about the racing school was that it was located in Philadelphia, so I had to come from Baltimore every Saturday to attend the classes from June to December 2013. But, I can say those trips were definitely worth it, and I owe a tremendous amount of gratitude for my father making those sacrifices for me to help me achieve my success.

The second program my father put me in was the National Youth Leadership Program. This was helpful in teaching me the values of leadership and government. I can be honest that as a teenager, I didn't like to embrace change, but when I reflect on these opportunities, they helped me grow as a person, and that's what any father would want for his son. The last point I will make on my father is he has found multiple ways to ensure a great life for my mother and me. An example would be in September 2012, during my junior year of high school when we went nearly the entire month without any electricity in our house. I will explain the details of that a little later. But as a bail bondsman, he was able to get a $500,000 bond to turn the lights on in our house. His phone was dying, and he had to go to his car to get a charge since he could not charge it in his house. He actually thought his phone had died and he missed the call, but when he heard the lady's voice on the phone, he was able to find the answer he needed to get us out of our hardship, similar to what he did when he was in his dry wash business.

While I was at Tuskegee in my orientation class, we were given the task of writing about our role model, and I ultimately wrote about my father. It was not only for a grade, but it was my way to thank him for all the hard work that he has done for me. If there is one sentence that I could say describes the relationship that I have with my father, it's that without him, there is no me. And without my mother, there is no me either, and I have to respect the balance of a parental relationship with a child. In ancient Kemet (Egypt), one of the concepts taught was Ma'at. One of the principles of Ma'at is balance.

This leads me to my final point of this chapter, which speaks to both men and women. To men, I will say you cannot use the excuse of not having a father in your life as to why you are not in children's life or why you cannot fulfill certain roles as a man because the universe will put some man in your life who can teach you the lessons you need to have. Plus, if you are man enough to make a child, then you have to take the responsibility to raise that child. To women, I will say unless there is a risk of harm to you or your child, you should not keep a man away from your child if he truly wants to be active in his child or children's life. The last thing our children need is to grow up with a poisoned mindset against someone who ultimately wants to be in their lives.

Children respect balance because there is no child who wants to grow up in a chaotic or dysfunctional home. We cannot continue the cycle of broken homes. If we do, then what are we teaching our children? That it's okay for a man to not be in their children's lives, or that it's okay to be an independent woman and that a man is never needed? That kind of thinking only leads to trauma for the next generations. Again, our children need the presence of a father to protect and provide for them, and they need the presence of their mother since the mother is the first teacher and a great nurturer. Above all, you need a great role model to help you in life, but it is important to return the favor to the next generation that follows. Remember, what goes around, comes around.

**"Two lessons that he passed along to his children. The first is that, no matter what, you never abandon your family. The second was that, no matter what, you love unconditionally. It is that kind of love that made my father the kind of father and the kind of man he is. He vowed that he would never walk away from his family and he never has."** - Donda West (from Never Abandon Your Family by Kanye West off "Donda")

# Notes and Insights

# APPRECIATE THE PEOPLE WHO ARE ALWAYS THERE FOR YOU

We have talked about having a great model, but never forget to appreciate the people who are always there for you. These people are basically the cheerleaders in your corner when you need them. I mentioned earlier that you should never take life for granted, but never take the people who support you for granted either. If you notice these two jewels coincide with each other. If you take the people who support you for granted, eventually they're going to wise up and leave you behind. There is value in having a support system because of the many benefits it has to offer such as the giving of advice, encouragement, and making great memories. Also, remember the people who appreciate you and want to be there for you want the same in return. It's a two-way street.

## The Value of Family and Friends

Family and friends are vital to your success. In fact, they are so valuable you can't put a price on them. Ask yourself, if you didn't have your family and friends, how would your life be right now? First, it would be lonely for sure. If a problem arose, you wouldn't have a support system to turn to in a time of need or the encouragement you needed to overcome that problem. At the same time who would be there for those milestones in your life such as birthdays, weddings, graduations, etc.? Family and friends are so important that the Bible makes mention of two scriptures showing how valuable they are which are Psalm 133: 1 ("Behold, how good and how pleasant it is for brethren to dwell together in unity!") and Hebrews 13:1 ("Let brotherly love continue.") With that said, there is great value in being with those you care about. Another place where I learned the value of family and friends is Kwanzaa, particularly the first day of Kwanzaa, which is Umoja or Unity. Umoja is to strive for and maintain unity in the family, community, nation, and race. Two of the biggest things I have learned is unity is needed for us to thrive and your family and friends are not just a group of people but a lineage that you should carry with pride. As my grandfather, may God rest his soul, would say, "**You come from good stock**." I want you to remember that for yourself as well: you come from great people in your family and friends. No community or race can thrive unless they come together and that's the value of having your family and friends.

Think about the joy you feel when you see your loved ones, friends, or anybody you appreciate come together for a cookout, weddings, holidays, or any celebration. It's an indescribable feeling. Even in the case of a funeral, you still need to come together to celebrate the life of the person who has made his or her transition, but to find peace and healing during the grieving process because no one should have to go through that alone.

And that leads to my last point on the value of friends and family which is you don't truly realize how valuable they are until they've transitioned. However, they're always with you in spirit, mainly through the memories you have created with them or the wisdom they have given to you over the years. As T'Challa (may he (our good brother Chadwick

Boseman) rest in peace) said Captain America: Civil War, "**in my culture, death is not the end.**" So always make sure you give your family and friends their flowers while they are still here.

**"Diamonds are forever like family and loyalty or real rap songs like C.R.E.A.M. or My Melody. Diamonds are forever like my infinite thought, like respect in the hood that can't be bought.**" - Gang Starr, "Family and Loyalty" (feat. J. Cole)

## My Experience with Family and Friends

All this mentioning of the value of family and friends, makes me reflect on the moments I have had with my family and friends. I can say I have been blessed to have many memories over the years with the people who have always been there for me. I mentioned the amazing work my parents have done for me particularly for my success in school. But I can also think about the amazing moments I have had with my friends over the years. For example, it's great that I can say that some of my closest friends are from elementary school and I can say it has been great to have them be a part of my journey. We have had a lot of great memories from graduating elementary and middle school together, going on vacations together, and celebrating birthdays.

One of the best memories with my friends was going to Orlando with my best friend Alpha in 2021 and 2022. Alpha has been my best friend since first or second grade and has been more like a brother to me. So in 2021, when he asked me if I was interested in going to Orlando, I was down. It was great because I hadn't been to Orlando since 2008. To me, it was one of those moments that I will remember for the rest of my life because it was with a good friend. It was so good we had to run it back in 2022. He has been a great friend to me and has shown this to me through his actions. For example, he'll call me to see how I am doing, or if my car is being worked on by my mechanic, he'll ask to see if everything is going well with my car. I always say if you have good people in your circle, keep them. I'll also add that because of Alpha, he's introduced me to another good friend, Dereje or D, as we call him. D has been cool as the three of us have hung out a lot, and through both of them, I am thankful to have two good people who I can have great memories with and go to for advice. Plus, we all have cybersecurity/IT careers in common, so that helps as well.

I can also say I have great memories with my family too. An example would be the moments they came together for my graduations. We celebrated weddings together and even had cookouts as well. The bottom line is family and friendship mean a lot to me as they should to you. Continue to make memorable moments that will last a lifetime! Other examples would include how I was blessed to meet a lot of people while at Tuskegee. There are two people I met at Tuskegee who I am proud to call my friends. Their names are Javanna and Genevieve. I've known both of them since our freshman year. At first, we all were a group of different people that we knew during our freshman year. We used to joke and say we were a part of "the Squad." I mean we would roll ten deep in the cafe. I still have great memories with "the Squad," but as you matriculate through your college journey, you start meeting other people and making new connections. We all did the same thing as well, but I appreciate that we kept our friendship throughout the years. Instead of being a "squad," we went to a trio. I can say we had some great homecomings and many other great memories as well. In fact, during their senior year and my non-graduating senior year, we had our monthly hangouts where we did various activities off campus such as going to the movies and karaoke.

One of my favorite memories of us is prior to their graduation while they were taking their graduation photos, the three of us took a picture together. It is actually one of my favorite trio memories because it represents our journey from freshman year to graduation. Plus, I have to shout a huge shoutout to Javanna. When I let her know that I was in the process of writing this book, she wanted to include it in her magazine. Anytime I can get support from my friends in whatever I do, that means a lot to me! As you go on your journey, it is great when you can take your friends with you and watch each other succeed!

## People Will Go In & Out of Your Lives, But Value Those Who Are with You Through Thick and Thin

One of the hardest jewels you may have learned in life is that not everyone you encounter stays in your life forever. Some people come into your life for a moment in time, and after the moment in time comes to end, you and the person go your separate ways. Many people experience this through friendships, relationships, and unfortunately sometimes, family members. The biggest thing is to take that heartbreaking experience and learn from it for the better. Also, do not take your pain out on other people who have nothing to do from the pain you're in at the moment; just because we live in a cold world does not mean everybody is a cold-hearted person. If you take your pain out on others, you are falling for the old adage that **"hurt people, hurt people."** The African proverb that summarizes this is **"The child who is not embraced by the village will burn it down to feel its warmth."**

What you have to realize is we meet multiple people on our journey of life, and I believe people come into your life for a reason. There is a lesson that can be learned from every person we encounter in life. Now a person should be vigilant in the people they give access to in their life, especially when it comes to friendship or relationships. Remember, not everyone is your friend or has the best intentions when they meet you. Some people, as I said earlier, are in your life for a moment or are friends for an occasion. In other words, some people are with you when times are good but not when the times get rough. If you want to see if you have a true friend, think back to a time when you were going through a challenge in your life, and if the person who you call your friend was there for you, then you're fortunate to have a true friend. In the end, your friends should be with you through thick and thin.

TLC said it best on their iconic song "What About Your Friends." "**If your friend is true, they'll be there with you through the thick and thin.**" That's the philosophy we should try to live by. I'm happy that I have friends who I know will be with me through thick and thin. I would do the same for them because it's the right thing to do. For example, I will never forget when my friends Justin and Amira helped me when my car broke down because of a broken axle. I had gone over a speed bump, and the axle broke. Luckily, I was in their neighborhood, and they were able to help me push the car to the side of the road and wait with me until the AAA tow truck arrived to take my car to my mechanic. I am thankful because I needed help, and I am glad that my friends could come through and give me a hand when I needed it. So, remember people may go in and out of your life but always appreciate the people who have shown you that they've consistently got your back no matter what.

## How Losing a Friendship Help Me Realize This Jewel

The experience that helped me realize not everyone you meet stays with you on your journey was when I had a friendship end with a girl who I had known since my freshman year of Tuskegee in 2020. Now before I get to why my friendship with her ended, let me give you the backstory as to what led up to this point. I met this girl my freshman year at Tuskegee as part of the squad I used to hang out with. In fact, I had met her and my friend Javanna on the same day. So, after eating dinner in the cafe on Friday night with some of the female friends of our squad, I went with them back to Douglas Hall, where a couple of them stayed to figure what we were going to for the rest of the night. Typically on Friday night both the guys and girls in our squad would figure out what the group wanted to do. So, while I am waiting for them in the lounge, they come out, and I meet one of their friends who I haven't met yet. She was from Houston, and not going to lie, beautiful as well. She was a little different than the other girls because she was a tomboy. To be honest, I had never heard or seen a tomboy actually. I thought all girls were your typical girly girls at that point of my life.

I will say she definitely made the tomboy look work though. Anyway, after that me and the rest of the squad including her decided to go and walk around campus. As freshmen, we hadn't seen the entire campus of Tuskegee yet, so it was cool to go on one of those freshman adventures. Now here is where my initial impression of her gets interesting. If you have ever been to Tuskegee, you'll notice past Henderson Hall and Milbank Hall, there is a road that leads up to what I believe is a goat farm if my memory is correct. Now there are no lights down that road, so it is pitch black at night. This might have been when Tuskegee was trying to do its "light the way" initiative to put more lights on campus. Well, let's just say the way was not all the way lit. So when we got to Milbank, my thinking was we'll turn back around because I'm not trying to go down a literal dark path, Ya boi just got to college, I'm not trying to come up missing. Well, this girl who I just met suggested we go into the woods.

I wanted to look at her and be like, "fam are you crazy?" Then the rest of the girls wanted to do the same thing, and oh yeah, I'm the only guy with them at this moment. Reluctantly, I went with them because I am not trying to have anything bad happen to them. It looked like something out of a horror movie. It was so black we had to use our flashlights on our phone just to see where we were going. Finally, we got to what looked like a house, and Javanna jokingly said we should go up to it. To which we were like "nah." And it was that point we all had regained our black cards back. Bet hey, looking back at it, it was a funny story, but I wouldn't do anything that damn crazy again. To all the incoming freshmen in college, don't be crazy like us.

Anyway, the girls who I met that night were pretty cool with each other the next few months. Then in November, everybody in our squad heard there was a Sadie Hawkins dance happening at Tuskegee. If anyone knows about Sadie Hawkins dances, that's when the girl asks the guy to the dance. So fellas, you really don't have much control in this situation, but if the girl asks you to the dance, congrats! I never heard a Sadie Hawkins Dance before, so I thought the idea was pretty cool. Plus, the dance was going to be the night before my birthday, so I thought that's cool. I mean I'm getting ready to turn eighteen, it's my first birthday in college, and I'm thinking that's going to be a lit weekend. I wasn't trying to just chill in my dorm that's for sure.

So as the dance was getting closer, a few of the girls in the squad had asked the guys to the dance. I was happy for them, but I was wondering if anyone was going to ask me to go, So the week and the dance happens, and I run into the girl from Houston at the cafe. After talking in the cafe for a while, I asked if she had asked anyone to the dance yet and if she was going. She let me know that she was actually going to ask me. I was down with it so I accepted her offer. Like I said, I thought she was cool, so I was glad she asked me.

Now, being that it was my birthday that weekend, she actually went into Tuskegee and bought me cupcakes. Now, where she went, I had no idea. But, the night before the dance, while I was hanging out with some of my friends, she texted me and asked me to come over to her dorm where she had a surprise for me. So when I came over, she surprised me with these cupcakes, They were good too, but I thought it was cool that she did that for me out of the blue, Looking back at it, it did mean a lot to me because I'm the type of person that is going to appreciate you when you do something nice for me, whether it's big or small. Needless to say, that definitely caught my eye.

The dance was the next night, and everybody in the squad was going to be pretty excited. Everybody was dressed nice and fresh, and it was a pretty good night. By the way, if you want to know how many people outside of us were at the dance, let's just say we were the dance. I'm not sure who was in charge of the dance, but I think it was the SGA. Don't quote me on that. But I will say that we made it work. Even though it was just us, it was a great vibe nonetheless. I'll say that it was one of my favorite memories from college. After the dance was over, we all went back to Douglass Hall and chilled for a while. Plus, it was only a few more hours until my eighteenth birthday, and you know some of my friends were trying to still hit me with the your still seventeen jokes before midnight. But it was all in good fun. So, after midnight came, and it was officially my birthday, I spent the rest of the night with the girl I went to dance with down in the Douglass lounge.

To be honest, I was still on a high from everything that happened that week from her asking me to the dance, surprising me with those cupcakes, the dance itself and it being my birthday too. We pretty much listened to 90s R & B in the lounge until about two or two-thirty in the morning. All and all, definitely a great night. With that said, I did let know that I appreciated her asking me to the dance. To be honest, it was at this point where I realized that I liked her for real. I was definitely seeing her as more than just a friend. I did go ahead and admit that to her, but we did decide to be close friends for the time being.

It was cool hanging out with her for the rest of the fall semester and even talking with her during the winter break. I was a little surprised when she told me in the spring semester that she wasn't coming back next year to Tuskegee. Looking back, I get it because college is not for everyone, and people should make decisions that are best for themselves. Still, it was sad to hear because I felt like I was just getting to know her and she was the first girl at college I liked.

Two of the last things we did together was go to Lake Tuskegee, which was the only time I went there, and walked around campus the day before she left to go back to Houston at the end of the semester. I went on to continue my Tuskegee, and she was back in Houston, eventually going to work on her art brand. Despite the distance, we still kept in touch. One of the things she did was make these small plaques of 24 and 8 in Laker colors for my birthday one year. I still have those mainly because those were Kobe's two numbers he wore in the NBA. Being that she was from Houston and a Rockets fan, I did get her a Rockets hat. This made sense to me because I have a Lakers beanie she used to like to wear, so I might as well get her something she could rep as well. Speaking of basketball, one of things I did like is that we had a common interest in watching basketball. It was mainly watching the Lakers play the Rockets and watching the events of the NBA All-Star weekend. If the Lakers didn't make the playoffs, we watched some of the playoff games the Rockets were competing in at the time.

In regards to the All-Star Game, we would choose who we wanted to win all the events from the celebrity game, rising stars game, three point, slam dunk contest, and, of course, the actual game itself. There's nothing wrong with a little friendly competition. She won some, and I won some; it was a fun thing we did for a while. One of things we also talked about seeing each other in Houston. I've always wanted to go to Houston because I heard great things about the city, plus I hadn't seen her since she came back to Tuskegee for homecoming in 2017. However, that was dependent on when the coronavirus pandemic was going to end since we were talking about this in early 2020, but I think we were both down to make it happen at that time. I can say I had great memories with her, and honestly, I didn't see us not being close friends. But life can definitely have other plans for sure.

Before I get to how my friendship with her ended, I did notice that something was different about her when we watched one last NBA game between the Rockets and Lakers. Of course, this is not too far in when the NBA had restarted their season in the bubble after the season was on hiatus for a few months due to COVID. So I was excited to watch our favorite teams go against each other, especially since nobody knew when the NBA or any sport for that matter was going to resume their season. The weird times of the pandemic, you feel me? So, the night before the game, I'd checked to see if we were still going to watch the game. She agreed and I was cool with that. So, when it was time to watch the game together on Google Meet, I was excited, but I could tell that she wasn't really in the mood to talk much. To be honest, the energy was just off, and it wasn't like any of the other times we watched games together. I get people go through things, but lowkey it felt like I was watching the game by myself. The Rockets won the game, but I guess my thinking was I'll talk to her when she's in a better head space.

Now let's finally get to how this friendship ended. About this time, I was wrapping up my last semester at Morgan State University to get my master's in cybersecurity. We were going to have our completion ceremony virtually due to the pandemic, but we could invite our family and friends to watch us. I had an idea of the people who I wanted to invite, and she was definitely one of them. In fact, she was the first person I wanted to invite. I tried to call her to invite her to my completion ceremony and didn't get a response, so I left her a voice message. Late that night, she called me back. At this point, I'm hoping she will be able to make the ceremony. Well, the conversation shifted into a different direction. She asked me what I thought of our friendship. I was honest and said that "it was something that I didn't take for granted." I meant it to because we had been friends for six years at this point. One of the things she pointed out was that she wanted her own space, but she wanted to go our separate ways. To be honest, I damn sure wasn't expecting her to say that. Looking back at it, it makes me wonder how I went from inviting her to my completion ceremony to her talking about our friendship ending. Forgive me for being brutally honest, but all I could think of was, "Where did that shit come from?"

I was shocked but also mad at the same time, so much so to the point I didn't know what to say really. It was moments of awkward silence on the phone. I do remember telling her I take friendship seriously. I also remember asking if she was going to do the same thing to her other friends, and she told me that wasn't any of my business, which in retrospective I get it, but in the moment of shock and anger I'm thinking, "well damn, am I the only one you're doing this to?" I just couldn't grasp the idea someone I really cared about would want to just cut me off like that. When the phone call ended, let's just say I went to bed mad and heartbroken.

A couple days had passed and the day of the completion ceremony came, and she texted me "Happy Graduation." By this point, I wasn't mad and had cooled off since I spoke to her that Saturday. I thanked her and I still wanted her to attend. I guess because I just wasn't ready to face the reality of what she said about the status of our friendship a few days earlier. Let's just say I was still trying to hold out on hope, but the thing about hope is it can be delayed disappointment. Needless to say, I didn't see her there. Don't get me wrong; I was happy to celebrate with my family and friends, but it's one of those situations where you really want someone to be there for you and they fail to come through for you.

So I called her later that night because I wanted to understand where she was coming from about our friendship and basically see what was up with her. Well, nothing changed. She reiterated she wanted her space, which to me made it seem like I never valued her space before. I mean there were times she and I would go periods without talking because I respected her space, and I realized she has a life. There were times I would ask how she was doing, and she didn't want to go into that. Plus, there was a period where she was in a relationship, and I obviously wanted to give her privacy. So to this day, her wanting her own space to justify ending our friendship just never made sense to me. I told her I didn't want our friendship to end, despite her wanting her own space and my ability to respect her right to her own space, but it was to no avail. After we ended the phone call, that was the end of our friendship, and we haven't spoken to each other since.

The lesson in all this is life will take you through the ups and downs and the highs and lows with certain people. But all you can do is learn from those experiences and appreciate the good times you have with those people, although that doesn't mean you forget the disappointment of you and that person going your separate ways. Also, remember we live in a big world, and you're going to meet a lot of people along your journey. You never know who you're going to have a great relationship, friendship, or connection with in the future.

And for the record, I have no ill will toward the girl who I lost a friendship with. I wish her the best of luck in her future endeavors. Like I said earlier, I know she was continuing to build her art brand at the time. I did buy one of her paintings for my dad as a gift when we were friends. What I realize is being angry or bitter isn't going to change anything between us. If anything, losing a friendship made me realize I am grateful for the real ones I still have in my life and to be thankful I have been able to build new connections as well. It's one of those look at the glass as half full, instead of half empty scenarios, you know what I mean? Honestly, that's how I've been able to find peace from that particular experience. It was a great friendship, and I can say I had a lot of great memories with her, but I knew I had to move on, and that is what I want for anyone who has lost a connection with someone they care about. If you keep reflecting on people from your past, you'll never see the people who you have the opportunity to build new connections with in your future. So yeah, people will come and go in your life. I saw a quote on Facebook that said, **Drive carefully on this road called "life", because people will switch lanes on you without a signal."** It might be hurtful and heartbreaking, but remember it's not the end of the world. You're still breathing, you didn't die. You'll be aight (or alright for my grammar police folks).

## How the Pandemic Impacted My Family and Friends

Flashback to New Year's Eve on December 31, 2019 for a second. Remember how excited everyone was for the start of a new year and a new decade? Everybody had an idea of what they wanted to do in 2020 and the moves they were trying to make in the new year. Now if someone told you there was going to be this crazy new disease called COVID-19 that was going to shut the world down for a period of time, you would have to socially distance from other people, wear masks, and not be able to see your family and friends for a period of time, you would think that person was crazy.

However, as we all know March 2020 came, and it was the year from hell. The world shut down, social distancing was the new normal; everybody had to wear a mask, and you couldn't see your family and friends for a while. Basically, a lot of us, myself included, took for granted that we could see our loved ones at any time before the pandemic. Once the pandemic hit, that changed. Remember, everything we did was virtual, and while it was cool that we had the technology to see each other, it wasn't the same as seeing each other in person. The pandemic was one of those scenarios where you don't know what you have until it's gone.

First and foremost, I do want to extend my thoughts, prayers, and condolences to those of you who did lose loved ones during the pandemic. My heart goes out to you all, especially when it was hard to come together to mourn their loss because of the COVID regulations. However, what I will say is for the family and friends we still had, it definitely made us appreciate the little things you had in life. For example, getting a phone call, text message, or Facetiming someone in 2020 just to see how they were doing hit differently than it did before, mainly because you didn't know when you were going to see them in person, but at least you knew they were good. If the pandemic taught us anything it is that nothing is guaranteed or promised. However, the pandemic was something we all needed each other to get through together, and it was a time we needed to lean on each other as family and friends, albeit six or more feet apart, we still needed each other's support in a time of chaos.

Plus, once it was safe to continue normal activities, it made you appreciate the fact you could see your family and friends again because, as the old saying goes, **"absence makes the heart grow fonder."** Life has a way of making you appreciate things you get back after you have lost them, and the pandemic was a perfect example. So now that we have come out the pandemic, or at least that what they've told us because I don't know if COVID is ever going to completely go away, be proud of the fact you were blessed to make it out of a tough situation and enjoy living your life with your family and friends again as you should. And yeah, let's hope and pray we don't see another pandemic in our future any time soon because those were truly some dark days having to hear the same thing on the news every single day. If anything, let's treat 2020 like a bad movie that doesn't need to be rewatched.

# NOTES AND INSIGHTS

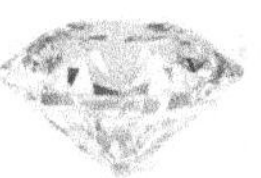

# CHAPTER 5

# DON'T LET OTHERS PUT YOU IN A BOX

What makes life interesting is that we all have different experiences, talents, dreams, aspirations, and goals. That also means we are going to have different paths as we navigate through life and shouldn't be limited. However, as you go through life, there are going to be people who limit your potential to one particular experience mostly to how they see fit. This is what I call having other people putting you in a box. When you let others put you in a box, you lose your light, spark, or uniqueness. In other words, you lose the one thing that makes you actually be you.

Let's think about a box for a second. It's rigid. You can only move so far within the parameters of the box. Now that's a literal box, but the same concept applies when we figuratively live our lives in a box. To be honest, one should not live their life in a box. You should have the freedom to go after the goals you want to achieve without limiting yourself to what you can or cannot achieve.

## The Importance of Traveling

One way to avoid being put in a box is to travel. Traveling has tremendous benefits because it allows you to see new places and gain new experiences. You never limit yourself to just one location because you aren't allowing yourself to see the whole world for what it is. Plus, the longer you limit your traveling, the more you start to think the world is only limited to where you are. It's cool to travel because you get a chance to meet new people as well as make memories that will last a lifetime. Plus, if you stay in one place for too long, it gets boring after a while.

The experience that made me realize the importance of traveling is when I went to Tuskegee for college. Now to be honest, Tuskegee was not my first choice to attend undergrad. I actually wanted to stay and attend college in Baltimore at Morgan State University. At that time, I thought Morgan was the perfect place for me to go to college. I thought they had a great engineering program, I had already met some of their students at the time as part of the AMIE program, and a lot of my classmates from high school went there as well.

I did apply to other colleges outside of Maryland as well, but to be honest I wasn't ready to leave Baltimore as weird as that may sound to some people. Up until that point, I had spent the majority of my life in Baltimore. I had been to other places outside of Baltimore to visit but not to live in for a long period of time. I just couldn't picture myself living anywhere else. However, my father was the person who put forward the idea of why it was important to go outside of Baltimore. In fact, I remember I was getting into schools down south, and my father telling me that "the signs were pointing south." Then it seemed that the signs were pointing to Alabama, which eventually landed me at Tuskegee.

One of many things I enjoyed at Tuskegee was that I was able to see what Alabama was like and make new connections with people as well. I admired that I got the full college experience going to Tuskegee as opposed to going to Morgan because I got a chance to know what it was like to live on my own and experience the campus life. Had I gone to Morgan, I wouldn't have lived on campus because I didn't live too far away from Morgan, plus I would be limiting my world to just one particular location. In fact, when I came back to Baltimore after my first semester at Tuskegee, I had asked if anything had changed around here, and the response was no. It was pretty much the "same old, same old."

Whenever I go to college fairs with the Baltimore Tuskegee Alumni Club, one thing I tell high school students is to consider the idea of going to school outside of Baltimore because of the benefit it has of not putting you in a box as far as seeing the world while telling them how great of school Tuskegee is. Remember we live in a big world, and your experiences should be abroad, not just one place. As Oliver Wendell Holmes, Jr. said, **"A mind that is stretched by new experiences can never go back to its old dimensions."** Once you see a new place and meet new people, you'll start to experience growth and you'll start wondering what else this world has to offer.

## Live Your Life By Doing What Makes You Happy

Part of not allowing other people to put you in a box is you should do the things that make you happy. Remember you only have one life to live, and you should live it to the fullest. Another point that you need to know is happiness comes from within and not always outside of yourself. Sure, other people or things outside of yourself can make you happy, but if you're not happy with yourself, does it really matter? It doesn't make sense if you are only doing the things other people say should make you happy or if you're doing the things other people find a sense of happiness in doing.

Now if you are doing something you do not find fulfillment in doing, you should make the necessary changes so you can have the fulfilling life you want because if what you are doing isn't making you happy, then you shouldn't continue to do it. An example of this could be that people who do not find fulfillment in their job or career and decide to do something differently. That could be they decide to go back to school or maybe go into entrepreneurship. In some cases, you have people who are satisfied in their career or job, but they may not be happy at the particular job they are located, so they may look for other opportunities elsewhere.

This belief in doing what makes you happy is why I never tell anyone they must follow a particular path to achieve success, because who am I to tell you how to live your life to achieve success? It is important to know that everyone's journey is different, so never think the path to success will be the same for everyone. For example, I appreciate what college has done for me, but I know college is not for everyone. For some people, their path may be trade school, the military, or entrepreneurship. The bottom line is I want people to be happy by doing what they want to do with their life, and I want to encourage you to find that sense of fulfillment in whatever you do as long as it doesn't harm yourself or others. That brings me to my next point.

## Always Encourage People to Go After Their Dreams and Goals

In life we have dreams, aspirations, and goals we want to achieve. Honestly, we believe we can achieve them. The only thing better than achieving a dream or goal is knowing you had people encouraging you to chase those dreams and goals. It's sort of like when you get to the top of the mountain; you feel a sense of pride knowing you got there. But you want to know you got encouragement along the way. The reason why you should encourage people to go after their dreams is twofold. The first reason is people usually don't forget the people who believed in their dreams and goals, and the second reason is you would want people to do the same for you. Like I said, what comes around goes around. If you know someone who has a dream or goal, and you are not encouraging them to go after those dreams and goals, you very well could be putting them in a box unless you have a specific reason why they shouldn't go after that dream or goal. In the end, always give people encouragement; they'll thank you in the end.

## Stay Away from Negative People Who Won't Allow You to Go After Your Dreams and Goals, or Who Say You Can't Do Certain Things

In addition to people encouraging you to go after your dreams and goals, you are going to have to face the unfortunate reality that there are some people who won't support you in going after your aspirations. Now sometimes it can be a genuine concern, which is understandable. But then again it could be because they had the same dreams and aspirations and were not successful at them. Or it could be, as I said earlier, average people don't like people who want to be more than average to do better than them. These are the type of people who will try to put you in a box.

The key is you should not let other people's criticism of you wanting to be better in life stop you. Remember it is better to try and fail than to not try at all. As Michael Jordan said, **"You missed 100% of the shots you don't take."** So whatever aspirations you have, you have to give it your best shot, otherwise you will regret the fact you didn't give it your all. Never be afraid to try. A$AP Rocky said it best, **"How you gonna knock somebody in the world for actually trying to do something? Trying. Since when has it been not cool to try?"** He actually went on to call that person a loser. I agree with that approach because if you are already admitting defeat and are afraid to try, then you do have a loser mentality. Never stop trying to reach your goals. As long as they're

SMART (specific, measurable, achievable, relevant, and time bound), you need to go after them.

Also, "**no one can stop you once you have decided to grow.**" I am not sure who said that quote, but it is true. So spread your wings and fly as well as shoot for the stars and aim for the moon because if you miss, you'll be among the stars.

## Everyone Has a Purpose

Another reason to not let others put you in a box is everyone has a purpose to fulfill on this Earth. What that purpose is, I can't tell you. That is something I hope you will find along your journey. However, I will say once you find that purpose, you should go after it with full force, whether it's to be a teacher, engineer, or activist. Also, it's cool to change paths once you find your purpose. An example might be that you have a person who has a career that pays the bills very well, but maybe their purpose might be to help others who are less fortunate, so they strive to find ways to better their community such as volunteering at a homeless shelter or offering a tutoring program for local students.

I will say once you find your purpose and fulfill it, you are living in your optimal self. Also, people will take notice. If you think about certain historical figures such as Booker T. Washington, Harriet Tubman, or Dr. George Washington Carver, they all had different purposes to fulfill while they were here. For Dr. Washington, it was helping improve the black community through education and economics by "lifting ourselves up by our bootstraps." In other words, teach us the value of self-help within our community by learning certain careers at Tuskegee and taking those careers within our community to benefit us economically. For Harriet Tubman, it was leading our people through the Underground Railroad to freedom from the horrors of slavery. Finally, for Dr. Carver, it was using science to change the world, mainly through the multiple uses he discovered for peanuts, soybeans, and sweet potatoes as well as being one of the greatest educators ever. What all three have in common is they walked in their purpose and their legacies are still honored to this day. In the case of George Washington Carver, his purpose is so appreciated that on his grave is the quote, **"He could have added fortune to fame, but caring for neither, he found happiness and honor in being helpful to the world."**

Plus, let's think about this: these three ancestors came up in the time of slavery and extreme racism. Had they not lived their purpose, we might not have heard about their great works we hear about today. So, live for your purpose because you may just inspire the next generation, and you can't inspire people when you're living in a box. As Tupac said, **"I'm not saying I'm gonna change the world, but I guarantee that I will spark the brain that will change the world."**

## My Ten Year Box

When it comes to my experience of being put in a box by others or myself, I can definitely think of a few examples. I can think of putting myself in a box by telling my dad I'd work at Walmart if I didn't go to college. I can think of others trying to put me in a box because at 6 foot 6 inches tall, people automatically assume I played basketball when in reality I was a swimmer. Although, I do enjoy playing basketball whenever I can, so I put my height to good use. For the record, just because someone is tall, doesn't mean they have to play basketball.

However, that doesn't compare to the box I spent ten years in my life in from 2003 to 2013. Before I go into the details of my ten-year box, let say something I am sure we all know. In life, people have different beliefs as far as religion is concerned. Now in some cases, you have people with religious beliefs that are different and extreme. When you hear about religions like that, what is your first assumption? Probably that this person is in a cult, right? Well, unfortunately, that's what I was in for ten years.

A cult is a box, an extreme box, one where there is basically no freedom. Actually, a cult cannot exist with freedom for its members because then it's not a cult. According to the Open Education Sociology Dictionary, a cult is defined as **"a relatively small group that excessively controls its members, who share set of acts and practices which require unwavering devotion, and are considered deviant (outside the norms of society), and typically led by a charismatic and often self-appointed leader."** The group I was a member of certainly fit these characteristics. Now to people who have never been a part of a cult, the misconception is they question how someone could be crazy enough to join something so ridiculous. But the thing is, nobody intends to join a cult. Usually, people are seeking for knowledge or enlightenment (like my parents were), or there could be a sense of vulnerability such as experiencing a loss of something such as a loved one or job.

So, in my case, my parents and I were Hebrew Israelites as members of the Israelite Church of God in Jesus Christ (ICGJC). The church had a few different divisions, and being that we were in Baltimore, we were a part of the Baltimore church. What led to us being in the church was that my father had stopped going to church for a few years. My mom would still go to church, and occasionally I would go to church with her.

In 2002, the ICGJC aired their TV show "The Hidden Truth" and introduced my parents to the church and their teachings. I think for my father it fascinated him that he had so many questions about the Bible that were getting answered. I think it was the same for my mother. To be honest, I didn't pay much attention to it because as a kid I thought religion was one of those things you did because of your parents. I was more into cartoons and playing with my toys than watching that.

At first, they did teach some great things, such as Jesus and the many of the characters in the Bible were black, there is a dietary law in the Bible, and even that so-called blacks, Hispanics, and Native Americans were the chosen people of God. After watching "The Hidden Truth" for a year, my parents decided to go to the church to attend their Sabbath service. By the way, that is another teaching of the Hebrew Israelites, that the Sabbath begins Friday at sundown to Saturday at sundown, instead of it being on Sunday as most Christians believe. We went to the church for the first time on June 21, 2003. I was six years old at the time. In fact, my reaction when the service ended was that it took too long. At the time, their services began at eight and ended at noon. As a kid, let's just say I was not interested in sitting in church for four hours. Then again, ask any child if they are interested in that, and I'll bet you money the answer is no although I'm sure there are some exceptions. As for my parents, their reaction was split. My father wasn't planning to continue to go to the church; he was content with watching their TV show moving forward. As far my mom was concerned, she actually wanted to go back, and my father didn't want her to go down alone. Little did we know that our lives would change for the next ten years.

As time went on, we did become members of the ICGJC. My father eventually joined their ranking structure, and we continued to follow their teachings. We eventually took on so-called Hebrew names as well; don't get me started on that foolishness because that was just a way of taking our natural identity. However, as time went on my father noticed there were some flaws with the church, and he had thoughts of leaving. But it seems as my father wanted to leave the church, the more ingrained my mom and I were becoming in it.

For me, as I spent time in the church the more genuine my belief became. I asked questions because I wanted to know as much as I could about the Bible. One of the questions I was asked was when I plan on joining the Hebrew Academy, which is basically their program to teach the brothers all their teachings and move up in their ranking structure. In 2011, I wanted to join, but my father had some concerns about my performance at school. My plan was to get through my freshman year Poly at and then join that summer since that was a transitional year for me.

I did join that summer. and when I reflect on that decision, it wasn't the best choice. I don't think I realized how different the church operates when you're in their ranking structure versus when you're just a member. The problem for me was I had put more emphasis on the ICGJC than I was with school. As a result, I wasn't putting the right amount of time into studying and my grades declined. That's what led me to being on academic probation and essentially having my father almost cuss me out for getting that letter from Poly my sophomore year. It was tough having to go through that because every day I went to school, it seemed like a struggle. In fact, this was the first time I had experienced depression. I had really lost my motivation to do well in school. But I honestly thought the church was going to be a way for me to escape that when, in reality, it was a hindrance. I even told my father the church was less stressful than school. It's sort of like how a person turns to drugs or alcohol to escape their problems. It may feel good for a moment, but doesn't solve the problem. All it does is put a bandage on the problem, but the problem doesn't go away. To say that I was naive was an understatement.

I didn't see a lot of flaws in the church as a child or as a member. In retrospect, it was when I joined the academy where I saw the flaws. One huge flaw was technically the brothers in the ranks had one day off if they were lucky. Most of the time was either spent attending classes during the week, unit work, doing security, or some type of activity to keep you busy and occupy your time. In fact, I find most cults tend to do that because the last thing they want is for you to get free from their control. Since I was in school, I didn't go to class during the week, but the problem for me was the weekend. Starting on Friday night being the start of the Sabbath. It was mandatory for us to attend church by 7 p.m. They were so extreme that if you were late, you'd be sent to council (in New York, mind you, where their headquarters were). Then, you had to come back on Saturday for a majority of the day until the late afternoon. Finally, if you were in the academy, you had to come back all day Sunday. This is what you call oppression at its finest. Now, I am a high school student, so I need time to study and do my homework. I might get some time on Saturday night, but I would also have to get ready for the Hebrew Academy on Sunday. Now on Sunday after the academy, in which we exercised, marched, and had class all day, I'd go home, shower, eat dinner, and then try to study and do my homework.

Well, it didn't work out the way I planned because I was so exhausted I would end up falling asleep and then waking up at about one to three in morning realizing I had fallen asleep. My dad would say that I would get so mad I wanted to cuss, and he wasn't lying. It felt like as soon as I was about to catch up on my school work, the weekend would come, and it would be the same routine. To be honest, I felt like a sixteen-year-old teenager going on fifty years old with all the stress going on in my life at the time.

The sad part about the church putting me in a box is I pretty much had to live two different lives. One life was trying to appear as normal as possible, and the other was trying to live the life the church wanted me to live. I would say being in a cult had more of an impact on me as a teenager than as a child because despite coming into the ICGJC at six years old I still had a decent childhood. I still hung out with my friends and family and did very well in school for the most part. Where it impacted me as a teenager was that I wasn't hanging out with my friends as much, I started doing poorly in high school, and I wasn't really involved in activities in high school. I wasn't dating anyone or getting to know any of the girls in high school. Then again, I'm pretty sure most sisters wouldn't have been down with the Hebrew Israelite thing. I mean try telling a girl you like, "I'd like to go out with you, but I'm never available on Friday night or Saturday, or Sunday for that matter." See how far that'll get you, my brothers. I don't think I did much socializing with my classmates due to all the drama going on my sophomore year, to be honest.

One prime example of the church affecting me in high school was I never went to the Poly-City game while I was there. The Poly-City is pretty much the biggest game between two high schools in Baltimore. So everybody and their mama was going to be there. Of course, my classmates were going to be there. I would go too except for one problem: the game was always on Saturday, and you already know where I was. Yep, the good old ICGJC. That's why I never went to the game from my freshman to junior year. Now I didn't go to the game my senior year, but it wasn't due to the church. I had actually been taken out of the church by my dad at this point, but I was a student in the Urban Youth Racing School, and their classes were in Philadelphia on a Saturday. I don't blame the racing school because I enjoyed the program, and it was a big part of my success today. In fact, I didn't go to any Poly-City activity until 2021 when I went to the tailgate and finally after thirteen years in 2022 made it to my first Poly-City game. Now that was due to a multitude of reasons: the ICGJC, the racing school, going to Tuskegee for five years, grad school at Morgan for one year, and COVID. But hey, better late than never.

I sometimes wonder if I ever got to fully experience being a teenager. In fact, the one regret I have about high school is I did not have a completely joyous experience. I enjoyed my last two years of high school, but as soon as I started to enjoy it, it was time for graduation. Looking back, I felt like I was trying to balance being a member of the ICGJC and school, and then trying to do so many activities to dig out of the hole I put myself in, that I don't think I ever got a chance to stop and smell the roses. I feel bad for young people who were born or grew up in cults like me because you're only going to experience childhood and adolescence one time. You're only going to experience high school once. It's sad when you think about it because when you're born or grow up in a cult, that is the only world you know, and it takes a while to blend into society after you leave. It's different when a person is an adult because at least they had an identity before they were a cult member. I think that's something not talked about enough honestly, which is the trauma and abuse people suffer in cults. The same way we need to address sexual, domestic, or child abuse, we need to address the fact that a lot of people have been abused in cults.

Another problem with the ICGJC was the financial burden it had on my parents and occasionally myself. Like a lot of churches, the ICGJC teaches their members to pay tithes. However, the difference between the ICGJC and the other churches is that the ICGJC requires its members to pay two tithes, which is twenty percent of your income. Now you would think with eighty percent of your income, you would be straight, right? Well, there are other payments you would have to make as well. Another required payment was their priest fund, which was $25 a week if you were in the academy and $31 a week if you were in the ranking structure. In fact, as a teenager, since I didn't have a job, I would sometimes ask my parents to help me pay the priest fund since I was asked about it by the church. Other payments would be for their high holy days, which would be $60 per person, and the Family Day Picnics and Israelite Summer Jams. If you were a brother in the ranks, you had to pay a garment fund depending on your rank, and that could vary from $200 to maybe $1,000. Finally, I cannot forget the infamous Dollar Drive to build "the cathedral from the ground up" using Isaiah 19:18-20 to justify giving money to support a cathedral being built by 2017, which never came to pass. Looking back at it, it reminded me of a joke Steve Harvey did on the church building fund where he said, **"Don't sit there and act like you ain't familiar with the building fund at your church. There ain't a black church in America that ain't got a building fund. We done had a building fund at my church since I was four years old, ain't put a doorknob on the damn church yet."**

So when you do the math, you are wasting a lot of money in this place. It's not just twenty percent of the money you're losing to two tithes, but actually almost, if not all, of your money. Other former IC-GJC members can verify this because a lot of them went through this same situation. The church was so money hungry that a lot of members couldn't pay their bills or get the necessities they needed to have a decent life. In fact, they would say you had to pay your tithes before you could pay your bills and use scriptures like Malachi 3:8 to justify that madness.

The sad part is the Bible would talk about how Jesus said in him we would have peace, and in the world, we would have tribulation. Of course, the ICGJC thinks the world is anything outside of their cult, but if this was the supposed church of God, then why were all the members in the church going through so much tribulation? In fact, a lot of the members, mainly the brothers, would say how "we all catching hell." But looking back at it, I was just too naive to understand how all these so-called righteous people could be catching all this hell.

Now as far as my parents and I were concerned, the financial burden of the church reared its ugly head the longer we were there. I can remember us having cars break down that we couldn't afford to fix and to us riding the bus for periods of time. There's nothing worse than you and your mom outside in the winter seeing three MTA buses go by that are not in service and hoping a bus will come soon to get you both out of the cold. But it was nothing compared to us struggling to keep our lights on in our house.

I can remember about 2011 until September 2012, we were running into issues when it came to paying the electric bill. I remember when we had to use curtains to cover up the fact we were using electricity at night, and unfortunately, the times when we did have our electricity cut off, we were having someone that wasn't from the electric company turn on our electricity, which was wrong on our part. It's hypocritical to act like you're holier than thou, but you're scheming and breaking the law just to have electricity. In fact, this should have been an indicator for us to leave the church. Then Labor Day 2012 came, which was a day I'll never forget. I was eating breakfast, and my dad was working on something at the computer, when all of a sudden, the lights went out in the house. We were both thinking at any moment the lights would come back on, but they never did. For the majority of the month, we had no electricity. Since we couldn't store food in our refrigerator, we had to use a cooler with ice just to store any perishable food we had. Since it was still hot outside, we couldn't use air conditioning and had to use the windows in our house. I couldn't do my homework at my house and instead had to go to the library. The fact that we had to use candles to light our house was sad but humiliating as well. I mean I didn't even feel like we were poor. We were "po." The difference between being "po" and poor is when you're "po", you can't even afford the o-r, that's how bad financially we were. It was like we were living in 1812 instead of 2012. Toward the end of the month, my father got the money to pay the electric company through a call for a bail since he is a bail bondsman. Later that week, he paid the bill. That Saturday, the lights finally came on and that nightmare was over. However, my father and I had to clean out one of our freezers. I mean the smell was awful; dead flies were in it, but that's what happens when you give all your money away and neglect paying your bills. That was brutal to say the least and something none of us wanted to go through again in life.

Another problem with the church was it had too much control over its members' lives. A main example was if someone was excommunicated or decided to leave the church, we were not allowed to have any contact with that person, which is something most cults do. In fact, the two of the craziest things I can remember them saying is you were going to hell if you left the church or you were a demon if you left. The other crazy statement they would say is, "cults keep you in, we kick you out." I remember telling my father that after he decided to leave the church before my mother and I did. He actually told me something I had never thought of at the time. He asked, "but Elijah how do they keep people in? By kicking other people out." That actually makes sense because if you're seeing genuinely good people all of a sudden get kicked out of your church and you're being told that if you get put out, you're evil and may be going to hell, from a fear mindset, you're going to do everything within your power to stay there so can keep your salvation.

Unfortunately, my mom was actually suspended from the church for a year. For what reason, I cannot remember. But I know my mom was never evil in the church. What was sad is no one could reach out to her because of the ridiculous order preventing people from doing so. It saddens me how the relationships built in there were conditional. You could only have friends there if you were in the church. Don't get me wrong; there were a lot of genuine people there. In fact, I am friends with a lot of them on social media now that they're ex-members, but it's sad all of us were controlled so much to the point where we would deny ourselves to have contact with people we may have had great relationships at one point because they were no longer in the church.

Another bad experience for me was in 2013, my last year there. It was a Sunday morning, and I was leaving Baltimore to go to New York because every three months the men in the ranks had to go to the church's headquarters for Major Conference. While we were there, we had certain men in the ranks get promoted to different positions in the church and give reports on the activities in the different churches in the region. I didn't get a new position, not that it really mattered away. But the event lasted way too long, emphasis on the word "too." I say that because I did not text my dad that the event was over until 3:47 AM! Now you're probably thinking to yourself, "Wait, you mean 3:47 PM right?" I wish, but no. Now, my mom was going to get me back in Baltimore when we got back. I was told that when my parents woke up the next morning, my father asked my mom where I was because I wasn't in my room. It's like it's early in the morning, do you know where your children are? Then my dad told me he looked at his phone and saw I had texted him at 3:47 AM letting him know we were headed back to Baltimore.

And when I tell you he was hot, he was hot. I mean my father was, as the late Robin Harris said, was **"pissed off to the highest level of pisstivity."** He told my mom I was going to be out of the Hebrew Academy. Once my parents came and got me from the church, my father told me I could no longer be in the academy. Let's just say this was the straw that broke the camel's back. Now I did ask my father if I had to go to school that day. Of course, I am thinking he's going to say no because I just got back to Baltimore and a lot of men were probably not going to work and their sons weren't going to school. In fact, there were men who lost jobs having to make all those trips to New York. I can remember my dad saying at one Major Conference that the leader of the church said that he didn't "give a damn about your job." My dad's thought on that was "he must not give a damn about me." He was correct though because the leader of the church, who proclaimed he was the Comforter the Bible speaks of, never did care about anyone in that place but himself. While I give him credit for being charismatic, like most cult leaders he was driven by money, power, and anything that would benefit him. Law 7 of the 48 Laws of Power is **"get others to do the work for you, but you always take the credit."**

The judgment of that is: **"Use the wisdom, knowledge, and legwork of other people to further your own cause. Not only will such assistance save you valuable time and energy, it will give you a <u>godlike</u> <u>aura</u> of efficiency and speed. In the end your helpers will be forgotten and you will be remembered. Never do yourself what others can do for you."** – Robert Greene, The 48 Laws of Power

Anyway, my father told me that I was going to have to go to school that day. Of course, I came to school late and exhausted. So exhausted, I started to fall asleep in English class. That was bad, but there's another part to this story that's even sadder. The day I had to go to New York was the same day as the Super Bowl. Now this Super Bowl was very special because it was when the Ravens battled the 49ers. One thing about me is that I am a diehard Ravens fan. When they won their first Super Bowl in 2000, I was four years old, so I have no memory of watching that game. My father did say, I had watched the parade, but I can't remember that either. So I was excited to finally watch my team play in the big game. But about two weeks before the game, it was announced we were having a Major Conference the same day as the Super Bowl. So unfortunately, I was not able to watch the game and see the Ravens win. I remember my parents went over to my aunt and uncle's house to watch the game with them and my cousin. I remember my dad showing the video of them celebrating the Ravens' win. I felt bad not being there. It felt like someone was missing there; it turns out that someone was me. In hindsight, I was robbed of a chance to experience one of the best days of my life. I knew the Ravens had won the Super Bowl when we were leaving New York, but it wasn't the same as actually watching that game live with my family. It was bad because a lot of the men in the Baltimore church had to experience the same feeling. Plus, any man in that place who enjoyed watching football couldn't spend the day with their families to enjoy the biggest football game of the year. Why? Because we had to be in New York for this stupidity and didn't leave until the early hours of the morning.

Later in the week, I had to let the church know I was leaving the academy. But, of course, with me having to go to church on Saturday, that also meant I would not be able to go to the swim team championships as well. I remember how bad it was having to tell my swim coach that I couldn't go to the swim championships. Even though I wasn't a star on the team, I still wanted to be there for my teammates and enjoy the moment. Thank God that happened my junior year of high school and not my senior year. So, I'm glad I had a chance to make up for that.

My time had come to an end with the church's academy, and a few months later, my father took me out of the church all together. Now that was a huge adjustment period. In fact, I remember after leaving the Urban Youth Racing School on Saturdays, I would start reading the Bible, and it wasn't because I wanted to; it was because my mind was still in the Israelite mindset. On the way back to Baltimore, my dad would ask me what I was reading. I told him Genesis the first chapter. His response was, "Boy, you don't know creation by now?" It's funny now, but I was only doing that out of a sense of guilt since I've been reading the Bible on Saturday for ten years. I mean here I was having fun on a Saturday, but I still had a need to read the Bible like I was doing something wrong. That's how powerful being in the ICGJC was.

Now my dad was trying to show me the flaws of the church, but due to cognitive dissonance, I wasn't trying to hear him. It came to a head when he sent me a YouTube video on "What If I Were Still an Israelite?". I was so mad at him that during my lunch break at the racing school I asked him why he sent this to me. His response was, "Boy, go back to class." My cognitive dissonance was so bad my dad would get into a lot of arguments with me. I told him I wasn't giving up my beliefs in the church. He wouldn't let me go to church events anymore, which I wasn't happy about. In fact, once my mom left the church later that year, I told both my parents I was going back to the ICGJC once I turned eighteen. I sometimes want to ask myself, "What was I on to make me say that?" However, that was to my parents' disappointment. It's that I couldn't let my beliefs in something so corrupt go; it was that I didn't want to let them go.

Mark Twain said it best: **"It's easier to fool people than to convince them that they have been fooled."** I remember my godfather telling my father I was "having too much fun to go back to that church." Honestly, he was right. The more fun I was having in the real world, the less I thought of the ICGJC. My dad had said my last few years in the church had caused me to lose my light or in other words my personality or identity. Around January 2014, I remember sitting with my dad in the living room and asking why he left the church. It was a great conversation. In fact, it was the first time we never argued. One of the things he suggested was that I watch documentaries on various cults in history, and I did. I realized these cults had a lot in common with the ICGJC. It was like my eyes were finally starting to become open. The last thing that helped me get away from the ICGJC was a video exposing the leader of the church and his lavish lifestyle. When I saw that I was disappointed because like so many other people I looked up to him in that church. It made me realize I was wrong all those years and what I believed in wasn't real. It was fake and a scam being run by a charlatan. However, it was just what I needed to free my mind from that madness I had learned for ten years. The truth hurts, but it's what you need to grow up, otherwise you'll be stuck in some fantasy land that doesn't exist.

Leaving a cult is a two-step process in my opinion. The first step is to physically leave, and the second step is to mentally leave. The second step is harder than the first because that's a process that takes time and usually doesn't happen overnight. It took me about eight months after my dad took me out of the ICGJC to free my mind from all that garbage because honestly I thought there was never going to be a time I would be in the church. I thought I was going to be there until either I died, or as the church put it, until Christ came back for his second coming. This was the only world I knew since I was six, going on seven, years old. I didn't realize I was in a box until I was seventeen years old, and I never looked back since mainly because as my godfather said I "was just having too much fun." After a while, I realized my father was only trying to help me and protect me from throwing my life away. Had I gone back to the ICGJC at eighteen, I don't think my life would be as good as it is now.

I am glad my parents finally left the ICGJC because in the years after we left it got worse and worse. In 2016, the church was raided by the FBI for financial irregularities. In 2018, the leader of the church and its treasurer were arrested for fraud and tax charges. Both plead guilty for using an entertainment company to take funds from the church members for their own benefit by spending $5.3 million on a lavish lifestyle without declaring the money to the government. So much for the righteous men of God. In January 2020, the leader was sentenced to eighteen months in federal prison, and the treasurer got twelve months and one day. They were also going to be under three years of supervised release. However, on April 1, 2020, the church leader died of complications of COVID-19 before serving his sentence. Unfortunately, there are people still there in that place. I have no idea why except cognitive dissonance is powerful. But I do hope they wake up and get out of that craziness.

I did have some great memories in the ICGJC, but it was time to move on for the better. I would say being in a cult is similar to being in an abusive relationship. It can start off great, but it will take a turn for the worst. You can have great times in an abusive relationship, but it doesn't take away the physical, emotional, or psychological abuse the other person is doing to you.

After the ICGJC, I did attend the chapel at Tuskegee because I was trying to fill the void left after I spent ten years of my life there. Now the chapel had nice people there and was a much better experience as compared to the ICGJC. But I eventually left because I am now more into spirituality than religion. The one thing I see in religion as opposed to spirituality is religion tells you what to think as opposed to how to think. Now I'm not saying people who practice religion are bad people. To be honest, I would say there are a lot of genuine people who practice various religions in the world, and yes that does include the Hebrew Israelites.

However, I believe religion is something that has to come from outside of a person whereas spirituality comes from within you. When you think about it, every religion has a doctrine its members must follow, and it is usually taught to us as children by our parents. That's not to say our parents are bad people; they were just teaching what was taught to them. That's why I say religion comes from outside of you instead of within you. I think once a person realizes they can travel along their own path without the need of a doctrine or religious leader and still have a relationship with the Most High, while finding purpose, peace, and fulfillment in their life, I would say that person is practicing spirituality as opposed to religion. Again, this is just where I am with my life, and it's through spirituality where after all these years I can find a sense of peace, especially from the craziness of the ICGJC. If anything, it's filled the void in my life left after being a Hebrew Israelite for ten years and helped me escape the ten-year box that was the Israelite Church of God in Jesus Christ.

But I will give you a bonus to this story: always listen to your intuition. Your intuition never lies. We have all had that feeling inside of us trying to warn us when something isn't right. and we've all made the mistake of ignoring our intuition. The irony is of all times I didn't listen to my intuition I can't think of a time it didn't backfire on me. The mistake we all make is that we trust our intellect over intuition. Our intellect tells us that we should give a person a chance, even though there's something off about their energy. However, your intuition is your spirit telling you this person doesn't deserve a chance. It's basically telling you yes or no. The reality is not everybody you come into contact with deserves a chance. Some people who mean you no good need to stay away from you as much as possible. The beauty about your intuition is that it basically looks out for you in any situation, and the more you listen to it, the better things can be for you. Honestly, had my parents and I trusted our intuition, we would have never joined the ICGJC, or at the very least, we would have left after the first time we went there.

If there's one thing I hate about growing up in a cult, it's the time I lost and can never get back. Time is your most valuable asset, even more than money. All the money we spent there, we have a chance to get back or make up for it. But you can't make up or get back time. Once the time is gone, all you can do is keep going forward, and that's how I look at this situation. Being raised in a cult, unfortunately, is a part of my journey. However, it doesn't define my journey. Hindsight is 20/20.

Oh and one last thing: if you do decide to join an organization (religious, business, social, etc.), make sure you do your research before you decide to join. The last thing I want to see from you is to join something that brings you pain, hurt, and regret. Join something you know not only makes you happy but have proof it can benefit you as a person. If you can find that and your intuition says that you should go for it, then do it.

## The Value of Freedom

If there is anything I want you to take away from this jewel, it's that you should be able to live the life you want without being restricted in a box. You should be able to make your own decisions and go after your goals without others holding you down from doing so. Never let people control your life to where you cannot do certain activities, careers, or think outside of the box they're trying to put you in at the time. It's okay to stand out from the crowd if that's what's best for you, especially if what the crowd is doing is not going to benefit you.

Now if people get angry at you for doing something that's different then what they're doing, then that's on them. In fact, here's something you may want to consider. In Amos 3:3 it says," **Can two walk together, except they be agreed?"** Now if you notice, there was no answer given to that question. It didn't say yes or no. By the way, don't take my word for it. Please look it up when you get a chance. Now as a Hebrew Israelite when I first learned this, I thought the answer was no. Mainly because I was brainwashed into thinking if anyone didn't agree with the teachings of the ICGJC, we couldn't agree with them. But now that I've gotten a little older and seen the real world, I realize you can still walk with someone and not agree.

As I said earlier, everyone's path in life is going to be different and ultimately, most people are trying to be the optimal version of themselves. When you think about it, it's going to be rare that you find someone who will agree on everything you do or think. You have your family and friends who may not agree on everything you do, say, or think. However, they're still your family and friends. Besides, who told you if you and another person don't agree on something, the two of you cannot walk together? It's actually a good thing we all don't agree on everything because if we did, we'd all be living in a box. What you have to remember is you are a human being, not a robot. You're not programmed to think a certain way and do certain activities 24 hours, 7 days a week, 365 days (366 for a leap year) a year. So again, never let others put you in a box. Remember, you're too unique for that, or as Pop Smoke once said, **"Be in control of your own shit, of your own creations. Know what I'm sayin'? Like be a creator. Like, I feel, like, when you create your shit, when you know whatchu want, know what I mean? Don't let nobody get in between you and your creation. If you want somethin', it gotta be that.**

In the end, it comes down to self-determination. This reminds of the Kwanzaa principle Kujichagulia, which represents self-determination through the ability to define ourselves, name ourselves, create for ourselves, and speak for ourselves. So, you have the ability to define yourself instead of others defining you, and that is what happens when you don't let others put you in a box.

# Notes and Insights

# CHAPTER 6

# THE STRUGGLE CAN BE A BLESSING

Life has its struggles and blessings, but sometimes the struggle can be a blessing. The jewel about a struggle is it can give you great lessons and opportunities. This can help you build character and allow you to be creative in overcoming a challenge. You'll be surprised how the toughest times in your life cannot not only make you a better person but can show you the abilities you've never had. As the old saying goes "**what doesn't kill you, makes you stronger.**" As Frederick Douglass said, "**If there is no struggle, there is no progress.**"

An example of how the struggle can be a blessing for me would be going a month without electricity in my house. Sure, despite how bad it was, the experience allowed me to get back on track with school. That was mainly due to the fact that no electricity meant no distractions for me such as television or video games. So all I could do at that point was study. In a weird way, it may have actually been what I needed because I was doing so poorly in school. I mean I was still in the madness of the ICGJC, but the results did pay off for me as I made the Honor Roll my junior year of high school, which was something I hadn't done since middle school. It actually helped to restore my confidence to be honest with you.

# You're a Different Person
# When You Overcome the Struggle

There's an interesting quote that says, "**Hard times create strong men, strong men create good times, good times create weak men, and weak men create hard times.**" The way I understand that quote is difficult times make people stronger and strength creates good times. However, being complacent in good times can hinder your strength and make you weak. That weakness will lead you to hard times once again and repeat the cycle. Overcoming your struggle gives you the gift of growth. Part of that gift is grit. Grit is having the courage and determination to push through no matter what the obstacles are.

When you overcome your struggle, you realize you are capable of being your optimal self. While it is great to go through good times all the time, that is not reality. Life has its ups and downs and its peaks and valleys. That means you will go through some rough patches. If you didn't go through the struggle, you would probably stay at the same level and not allow yourself to grow. It would be like if you were in high school, and your math teacher was still teaching you that 1 + 1 = 2 instead of teaching you algebra.

Finally, going through the struggle can help you be the person you are today because it is going to give you the lessons of how to be better. It certainly has for me, and I'm sure you can think of plenty of examples in your life whether it was school, work, or whatever situation you were going through, you were able to overcome a struggle and be a better person. I heard Dr. Ray Hagins mention in his lecture entitled "What Makes You Think That Your Life Will Be Better?" the "10 Steps for Experiencing A "Better" Life". Step 3 was "**Understand and accept that pain is a natural progression of life**". This is actually where you get the term growing pains. An example of this might be in sports where you have a team in rebuilding mode that hires a new head coach, rebuilds through the draft, and plans to have their team in contention to win in the future. Well, there are going to be growing pains involved. They may deal with rookies and undrafted players. They may have games where they almost find a way to win but come up short. There may be years where they don't make the playoffs. However, as the years go by, they start getting better and better as they keep building their team and eventually become a winner. The same applies to your life. You are going through rough patches, but eventually you will progress. DMX said it best, **"See, to live is to suffer, but to survive, well, that's to find meaning in the suffering."** I honestly didn't understand those words until he passed away. What I take from that is: once you overcome or survive your struggle, you found the lesson was meant to be learned from that struggle, which allows you to grow.

## A Setback Is the Perfect Stage for a Comeback

As much as we would like for it to be, success doesn't always come quickly. It can be a tough process that will have some setbacks, but a setback is a perfect stage for a comeback. A setback allows you to go back to the drawing board and plan on how to get better moving forward. Another thing to note is to not judge yourself because you aren't seeing success right away. It doesn't matter when you achieve your success as long as you achieve it. Your success will come as long as you continue to put the work into achieving your goals.

**"Success is to be measured not so much by the position that one has reached in life as by the obstacles which he has overcome."** - Booker T. Washington

Also, remember you can bounce back from your setback as well. The important thing is to never give up and keep trying. Confucius said

**"A man is great not because he hasn't failed; a man is great because failure hasn't stopped him."** In other words, a setback doesn't stop you from being great; it's the commitment to excellence that makes you great. Part of that commitment is to not let failure stop you from achieving your goals. Sports is a microcosm of this because a team that has a goal of winning a championship is going to lose some games in their season usually, but they don't let those losses stop them from their goal of winning a championship, even if it takes years to accomplish. So, it doesn't matter how long it takes you to win, as long as you win, they can't take it away from you. As Al Davis used to say when he owned the Raiders, **"Just win baby!"** Although, I don't think he'd be saying that much now since the Raiders haven't consistently won in recent times, but hey, keep hope alive Raider fans, your day will come someday.

## The Struggle Can Be Frustrating, But It Doesn't Mean It Will Last Forever

We have often heard the saying that "nothing lasts forever" when we're talking about something good. However, the same can be applied to the struggle. As frustrating as it is, the struggle doesn't last forever. As I said earlier, you are going to learn a lot about yourself when you overcome a struggle. I would argue you can learn a lot more about an individual when times are bad as opposed to when times are good. You can learn is if the person is a fighter or a quitter. Another question is what is the person's character? Do they continue to work hard to solve the problem, or do they use nefarious ways to get ahead?

Minister Farrakhan stated in a tweet in 2017 that **"We cannot go through life without pain. We cannot go through life without difficulty. We cannot go through life without struggle. God has ordained this because these are the circumstances of life that manifest the** quality of our character, our heart, the core of our being." To summarize what the Minister tweeted, you are to have moments of pain, difficulty, and struggle in life. However, these circumstances mold you into who you are. As Dr. Martin Luther King, Jr. said, "**The ultimate measure of a man is not where he stands in moments of comfort and convenience, but where he stands at times of challenge and controversy.**" Remember, complaining about your struggle doesn't solve anything. All you can do is figure out a way to overcome your struggle and take action.

On his song "Part of the Game", 50 Cent says it best: " **I know heartbreaks, setbacks…if I crap out, I'm sure I'ma get back. I been through the ups and downs, you know I get around. So to me, it's all a part of the game (ah, yeah).**" Then again, if there is anyone who knows about the struggle, it would be 50 Cent. We're talking about someone who was shot nine times and was able to survive and have a thriving career as a rapper and businessman. So never let anyone say you cannot bounce back from your struggle. As long as you have breath in your body, there's always a chance to overcome your struggle.

## What the Pandemic Taught Us About the Struggle

The pandemic was the definition of a struggle because life as we knew it changed. However, despite that universal struggle, some people did find blessings within the struggle. One blessing might have been that some people had time to focus on passions they may have always wanted to pursue without any distractions. Some people may have found new ways to make money after losing their jobs. An example was when the pandemic first hit, some people decided to make and sell masks to have a source of income. However, I would say the people who show the best grit and determination were the students who graduated from whatever level of school. It had to be hard to transition to virtual learning at the time, but many students didn't let that stop them from finishing their studies. Plus, let's not forget the protests against police brutality going on as well. As we were in the midst of two pandemics at the time, and the world around us changed, you still have people who were able to achieve their goal of graduating and making a future for themselves. It goes to show that despite the struggle, people are still able to do anything they put their minds to. With that, I'll raise a glass to you all!

# NOTES AND INSIGHTS

# CHAPTER 7

# Always Give Back and Help Others

When you make it to being your optimal self, you should think about who is coming behind you. Effective leaders don't necessarily have followers, but they are building leaders to come behind them. For this reason, it is important to always give back and help others. By doing this, you're helping the next generation be able to get to their optimal self with the lessons and opportunities you have been given. If you have been given a gift, then you should share that gift with the world. It goes back to when I said you should have a great role model. Well sometimes, you need to be a good role model as well, and that starts by giving back and helping others.

## Why I Give Back and Help Others

The reason why I give back and help others, besides it being the right thing to do, is because I think about my own journey and where I'd be if I didn't receive the help I did to succeed. My journey wasn't easy, and I can say I know what it's like to feel lost on the road of life. I graduated from high school with a 2.58 GPA, and I wasn't sure that I'd be blessed to achieve some of the great things I have done. I don't take that for granted.

Part of the reason I was a tutor in undergrad and graduate school because I received tutoring from AMIE when I was in high school, and they played a big part in turning my grades around. I didn't want to see students struggle academically like I did. In fact, when I got to Morgan for grad school, that's what made me want to be a tutor with AMIE.

Once I graduated from Tuskegee, I became a member of the Baltimore Tuskegee Alumni Club and joined the recruitment committee. I appreciated what Tuskegee and, more importantly, BTAC did for me as far as me getting to Tuskegee and having a great college experience. In addition to me telling Baltimore students about Tuskegee, I also tell students who may have a GPA slightly under a 3.0 that they should still apply to Tuskegee especially when they gave me a chance with a 2.58 GPA. Applying for college can be a very exciting but anxious process. As a person who's been through that process, I want to give the students the best advice possible. I believe when you have been given opportunities to succeed, at some point you have to help give other people those same opportunities.

## The Flaws of a Selfish or "I Got Mine, You Get Yours" Society

In life, you can't always care about yourself. There are moments where we have to care about other people. A society cannot thrive if everyone has a selfish mentality. The best way to survive is as a collective. This is put into practice the best through Ubuntu. Ubuntu is I am because we are. Nobody wins when the family feuds. When everybody is selfish, that leads to division and makes it harder for people to stay together. What makes great societies or cultures great is they find ways to help others instead of only helping themselves. In other words, they know the importance of helping their society succeed for the better. An example of this may be when people within a society agree to do business with each other and by doing so, that allows them to create wealth within that society, which they can use to help their families and create more opportunities down the road.

One of my favorite quotes by Booker T. Washington is "**If you want to lift yourself up, lift up someone else**." The jewel with that is instead of focusing on how to lift yourself, the focus should be on how to lift other people because in doing so you will lift yourself. This is what people do to help others succeed. Selfish people don't do that as they only intend to lift themselves. An example of this for me was when I was in the ICGJC, and the leader of the church was financially exploiting the congregation to his benefit and leaving so many members financially desolate. The reality was everybody should have been uplifted, especially since we were supposed to be so godly. In the end, I will say you do have to look out for yourself because if you're not good, how can you help other people be good? However, don't use that as a crutch to prevent you from looking out for other people because that can backfire.

## The Golden Rule

When it comes to helping others and giving back, it can be simplified by the golden rule, which is as we all know: "**do unto others as you would have them do unto you**." It makes sense because the way you would want someone to treat you is the same way you should treat others. The key we have to realize is we should never think there won't be a time where you're going to need help. As I've said multiple times, everything in the universe boils down to reciprocity: what goes around, comes around. It's important to "**be humble and never think you are better than anyone else. For dust you are, and unto dust you shall return**." I am not sure who said that quote, but that is definitely a jewel.

I would also say when you follow the golden rule, you should feel good knowing you were to help others because you never know how your action may have been a blessing for somebody else. It could even be something as small as offering encouragement to someone going through a tough time. I will elaborate on that a little later, but to quote Booker T. Washington again, **"The happiest people are those who do the most for others."** When you're happy with yourself, you don't mind doing things that help others. In my opinion, a lot of people who are selfish most likely have something with themselves they are not happy with. I'm not a psychologist, but that's my thought process. I would say if you truly want to experience happiness, find ways to help others. You'll definitely feel great about yourself. Another benefit of giving back and helping others is that it shows you have great character and you value other people as opposed to yourself. When it comes to character, we are speaking on your morality and how you operate with other people.

**"Character, not circumstances, makes the man."** - Booker T. Washington

## People Who Are of Good Character Themselves Appreciate What You Do for Them and Remember Your Deeds

Going back to when I said that your actions may have been a blessing for somebody else, people who are of good character will appreciate that and remember your good deeds in the long run. In fact, they are most likely to repay the favor. Notice how I said people who have good characters themselves will appreciate you because I am sure we all have done things to help someone who we thought had good character and it turns out we got the opposite. An example of this may be when you let someone borrow money from you and when you expect them to pay you back, they refuse to do so. Trusting people with poor character happens to the best of us. It's a learning experience, and as you get older, your intuition will tell you who has good character and who doesn't, and you'll be less likely to help those with poor character qualities.

Another thing to take note of is the importance of having a good name. The Bible basically states that a good name is better than riches. One thing about a good name is it's your legacy. Your legacy is what people will have left of you after you transition. Being selfish doesn't help your legacy. The last thing you want to do is have a bad name or reputation. When you look at some of the most famous people in history who have passed on, their deeds in helping others are still talked about to this day. Even people who aren't famous who have passed on who did things to help others have their deeds are remembered. An example of this would be your loved ones who have made their transition. Dr. King said it best: **"Everybody can be great because everybody can serve."** So, it is important to give back and help others because when you leave this Earth, that's what people are going to remember you by. Serving and helping others allows you to achieve greatness because it's not something hard to do. As Dr. King said, **"You don't have to have a college degree to serve."** I would say if you can find something that makes you happy that can help others, go for it and achieve your greatness! You never know who will remember you for it. As Dr. King taught us, **"Life's most persistent and urgent question is what are you doing for others?"** So yes, it is good to look out for yourself, but take time to think of others along your journey because it shows growth in your character, and you will definitely stand out to other people who have good character themselves. Also, when it is all said and done, do you want to be remembered as only being interested in helping themselves or as a person who helped others along their journey? Ultimately, that's the decision you're going to have to make.

## Everyone Needs Help Along the Way

A big jewel we learn in life is we cannot get to where we want to be in life with help. A lot of people love to say, "If you want something done right, you have to do it yourself." We all have thought like that. But to be honest, there are going to be moments in life where if you want something done right, you are going to require some help. It reminds me of another saying, "**Measure twice, cut once**." Well, sometimes when you measure twice, you may require some help.

A great example of this is sports. What I like about sports is that it is a microcosm of how society works. Sports teach you how to work as a team toward a common goal, which is to win the championship. In life, it is the same philosophy. You have to work with others in your career, school, or a business. Life ultimately boils down to relationships and how you treat others. This doesn't mean you have to have a huge quantity of relationships, but it does mean you should have quality relationships with people if you wish to succeed.

Going back to sports, even the greatest players need help. For example, Michael Jordan is arguably the greatest NBA player of all time. Most people will point out the fact that he won six championships as a reason why along with any of his accolades. However, many Michael Jordan fanatics forget there was a period early in his career where he couldn't win a championship. Now it wasn't because Michael wasn't a great player; it was because Michael had to learn the importance of having a great team around him. Phil Jackson did a great job teaching him that when he taught the Bulls the Triangle Offense and the importance of passing the ball. Michael never stopped being great, but he still had to utilize his teammates Scottie Pippen and Dennis Rodman to help him win championships because after all it's a team sport and there is no I in team. Of course, this was on full display when we saw *The Last Dance*. Great players are tremendous, but it's better to have a great team. When you look at the history of team sports (i.e. basketball, football, soccer, baseball), can you think of a player who single handedly brought their team to a championship? Probably not.

The same applies to your life. All the success that you have achieved over the years, did you achieve that success by yourself or did you receive help along the way? There is nothing wrong with receiving help in life; receiving help makes you better. If you're against receiving help, then it goes back to your ego being a problem like I discussed earlier. Besides, if you ask any successful person whether in academics, sports, or business, they will tell you they had to get some help to be where they are today. In the end, I'd rather receive help than to receive hell in life because if you don't get help in your life, you might as well remove the p off help and put an l on it since that's what you're going to go through.

# Notes and Insights

# POSITIVITY IS GOOD FOR THE SOUL

On your journey, you're going to have your ups and downs, highs and lows, and peaks and valleys. However, it is important to remain positive, especially in the toughest situations. On Instagram, I follow Dr. Alan Mandell, who's IG is @motivationaldoc, and he posted that you have to "**train your mind to see the good in everything. Positivity is a choice. The happiness of your life depends on the quality of your thoughts.**" This brings me to the first point on this jewel.

## You Attract What You Are

Using the last part of Dr. Mandell's quote, "**The happiness of your life depends on the quality of your thoughts**" basically means you attract what you think. A lot of people like to say "**As a man thinketh, so is he**" which paraphrases Proverbs 23:7, which states "**For as he thinketh in his heart, so is he.**" If you train yourself to think positively and see the glass as half full, then you put yourself on track to live a great life. However, if you train yourself to think negatively and see the glass as half empty, then you put yourself on track for a life that isn't living to your best potential.

A lot of people like to use affirmations and the power of manifestation to attract what they want. Affirmations are good in the sense that they train your mind to think positive thoughts. So telling yourself things such as "I am beautiful;" "I deserve to be loved," or "I am capable of doing this task" definitely goes a long way. The key is it starts with the mindset. A positive mindset can produce positive results. A negative mindset will produce negative results.

Examples of a negative mindset would be statements such as "I will never be successful in my career," "I will never be financially stable," or "I will never lose weight." The result of these negative mindsets would be you won't be able to achieve any of the goals you want to achieve. Having a positive mindset will give you the motivation to go after what you want to attract. Now remember, having a positive mindset is only the beginning. You have to put the work in to attract what you want. As the old saying goes, **"faith without works is dead."** You can't say something such as "I will be a successful entrepreneur" but never research how to start a business, how to improve your business, or determine what product you want to sell first. You can't say "I'll lose weight" but all you do is eat unhealthy foods all day. Remember, you are what you eat. You can't play a sport and say you want your team to win a championship but if you don't go to practice.

The formula behind this is simple: Positive mindset + action = positive results, or it could also be positive affirmations + actions = manifestation, depending on how you look at it.

I'll apply this formula to myself in the sense that this is the first book I have ever written, and at first, I didn't plan on writing a book because I just didn't think it was something I could do, nor had I thought about. But as I thought about how I wanted to write something that could help and inspire others, it led me to write the book you are reading now. So, the affirmation for me was I was going to write a book sharing the lessons I have learned in life and how it could inspire others. The action for me was to outline the lessons I wanted to discuss, and the manifestation was the book you are reading now. Remember, the energy you attract is the energy you give off. It starts with your mindset and the actions you do. Once you do that, you'll be able to manifest your goals.

**"If you can see it, in your head, if you picture it, if it's clear…then it is a possibility. If you believe in it, it's already happened, you just haven't gotten there yet. You have to learn how to recognize things and you just have to know what road to take to get to your final destination because a thought, just a thought form can manifest itself into physical form. So, it's all about believing in yourself, believing in what you do, being able to see it, knowing how to get there, living it and trust me it'll happen. Ask and ye shall receive, that is a very true thing." - Lisa "Left Eye" Lopes**

## The Benefit of Positive Energy
## as Opposed to Negative Energy

One of the benefits of positive energy we discussed earlier was it puts you in a positive mindset, but they're other benefits to positive energy as well. Going back to "you attract what you are," one benefit is if you have positive energy, you will attract people who have positive energy. People tend to want to be around like-minded people. Great minds think alike. Another benefit is your positive energy can influence other people as well, especially if those people are going through a difficult time. That's when they are going to definitely need inspiration to uplift them. The ultimate benefit of positive energy is that it's healthy. It keeps you upbeat and, in a way, makes your light shine bright. Believe me when I tell you that people are always watching you, and I don't mean that in a sense of paranoia but more in the sense that people are always taking note of you even when you least expect it. As Kendrick Lamar said on "Count Me Out." **"Good energy in the room, drop the location, please."**

## Peace Is One of the Greatest Gifts to Have

One of the greatest joys of positivity is it brings you a state of peace. Ultimately, we all strive to make our lives as peaceful as possible. Without peace, there's chaos. One of the things I've heard my father say a lot is how he hates chaos. I remember growing up, he would get on me if my room wasn't clean by saying, "If I couldn't keep my room clean, how could I keep a house clean?" Another thing he would say is to "put things back where I found it and the way I found it." To be honest, as a kid, I thought he was being picky and overbearing. In fact, when we were with the Hebrew Israelites, some of the men thought my dad was picky because he would say things such as, "You know how picky he is," especially when it came to cleaning the church or when they would ask him to proofread their reports. They ask him what was wrong with the report, and he would respond by saying, "Everything." or "I wouldn't turn that in." Let's just say while some of the Israelites, or as he likes to call them "the Ignorites," meant well, unfortunately some of them weren't the sharpest knives in the drawer.

However, the lesson my father was trying to tell was if your life is chaotic, it will reflect in how you live and how you operate. Generally, people who are in a constant state of chaos are typically avoided by people who are in a state of peace. If you find that your life is chaotic, then you need to find how to make your life as peaceful as possible. In the end, chaos leads to stress. That stress is going to take a toll on you mentally and emotionally. As Tupac said on "Changes," **"We gotta make a**

**change. It's time for us as a people to start makin' some changes. Let's change the way we eat. Let's change the way we live and let's change the way we treat each other. You see, the old way wasn't workin'. So it's on us to do what we gotta do to survive."**

Also, when it comes to peace, a few years ago some people were saying things such as "be his peace" or "be her peace", especially when it comes to relationships. I get it because everyone wants to be in a relationship that's peaceful or hopes their significant other brings them peace. It's like how people say they want to be with someone who makes them happy. Here's what I'll say to that, as great as that sounds, you should be striving to be your own peace. You don't have to depend on other people for your happiness or peace. Don't get me wrong; I'm not saying other people can't bring you happiness or peace. I'm saying you shouldn't solely depend on other people to do that because the same people who you think will bring you peace and happiness can also take that away from you if you give them too much power. There are a lot of wolves in sheep's clothing in the world. Also, if you haven't been doing the work to bring yourself peace, is it really fair to put that responsibility on someone else, especially if they have been doing the work to have peace? If you're in a chaotic state, it's going to be hard to bring a peaceful person into your life. In other words, you have to learn to heal first and make the necessary changes first.

Your peace is like your life; you have to defend it at all cost. If someone you know is bringing you chaos or toxicity, you may have to distance yourself from them. Above all, you need to be at peace with yourself, and if you're not, you need to do something that helps you get to that peace. For example, that could be therapy, meditation, prayer, fasting, journaling, exercising, etc. So yeah, being his peace or being her peace is good, but when you can be your own peace that's even better. It's okay to be by yourself and work on yourself, and I'm pretty sure someone who's at peace with themselves will take note of that and who knows, maybe at that point, you both might be able to be each other's peace.

## The Consequences of Negative Energy

So we have heard about the benefits of positive energy; now we can discuss the consequences of negative energy. The first consequence is those with positive energy are going to avoid you. It's similar to if you had a room full of healthy people, and one person who has a contagious disease comes into that room. It'll only be a matter of time before that person infects the other people in the room. The only way to not get sick is to socially distance yourself from the infected individual until they get better. The same applies to someone with negative energy. The person is going to spread their negativity to those with positive energy. Now those people are infected with negative energy. It's hard to live your life with people who always want to be at a low vibrational frequency and you're trying to operate at a high vibrational frequency.

The second consequence is not only are you hurting others with your negative energy, but ultimately you are hurting yourself. There is no benefit to having negative energy. When you walk around with toxicity, you need to think about how that is supposed to help you. All you are doing is showing why others shouldn't be around you. If you are carrying negative energy and you find people are distancing themselves from you, then you need to look in the mirror and make the changes you need because it is not other people who are the problem: it's you.

# Remaining Positive Can Help In Even the Toughest Situations

The key concept of this book is to be your optimal self, even if that means you have to go through tough situations. The main objective you want to understand is you have to remain positive in those tough situations. Tough situations create challenges, and you can either rise above those challenges or drown in them. To rise above those challenges, that's going to require positivity. You can't cry over spilled milk, and being negative won't solve your situation. If you think about any situation that was tough for you, you had to be positive to get through it. Otherwise if you are negative, you may be still going through the situation. What can also get you through a tough situation is knowing you have been able to overcome previous challenges. Experience is always a key factor that can give an extra layer of positivity for you. Life is going to have its challenges, and they're going to happen at any moment, but positivity is good for the soul, and I wish you nothing but good vibes along your journey!

# NOTES AND INSIGHTS

# FOCUS ON THE JOURNEY AS OPPOSED TO THE DESTINATION

Going back to the quote I used from Left Eye from the previous chapter in which she said, **"you just have to know what road to take to get to your final destination…,"** brings me to the ninth jewel in your journey, which is to focus on the journey as opposed to the destination. Well, the **"road to take to get to your final destination"** is the journey. The journey is the roadmap to your destination. It's the plan to help achieve your goals, similar to how in sports a team has a game plan to win a game. The destination is for the team to win the game, and the journey involves practice, team meetings, film sessions, etc. It's great to get to your destination, but don't forget to enjoy the moments along the road to get to your final destination, because that's where you discover that your jewels are in your journey.

## It's a Great Opportunity to Reflect and Appreciate the Moments

One benefit of focusing on the journey as opposed to the destination is it is a great opportunity to reflect and appreciate all the moments that got you where you are today. When you get to your destination or goal you have for yourself, there are going to be a lot of moments you will have along the way, whether they be good or bad. It's sort of like your life is one big road trip, and the moments you create are like stops along the way, or how when you're on a vacation and you embrace the atmosphere of the place you are in as you go to the various places in that location. The beauty of reflection is it allows us to hit the pause button and analyze how we should move forward. In terms of appreciating the moments along your journey, it basically goes back to stopping and smelling roses. Sometimes, I think we get so caught up in reaching our destination or goal that we don't appreciate the moments along the way, or celebrate the small victories as we inch closer to our goal.

Using myself as an example, I'll go back to my time in high school. Again, that was an interesting and, to be honest, crazy time in my life. But I think because I was so focused on what I was going to do with my life after I graduated high school I didn't appreciate all the moments that were great like I do now. I think when your life is in a state of stress and confusion, it is hard to stop and appreciate the moments you create. Trying to get my grades right and doing a bunch of extracurricular activities to get to college put me in a what's next mentality. Basically, it was like, "Okay, I'm on the swim team; I'm a part of Spanish Club; I'm a part of AMIE; I'm going to Philly for Urban Youth Racing School; I'm a part of NSBE: Is there anything else I need to do?" Honestly, it felt like I didn't have much time to relax, take a breath, and take everything in as much as I wanted to. Then again, if things were different, maybe I could have.

However, now that I'm in a different place in my life, I've learned to appreciate every moment I have. A perfect example would be when I catch up with my high school classmates whenever we have our class outings every now and then. It is a great opportunity to see how the fam is doing. In other words, it's a way to take a break from all the everyday activities we do. In fact, when I got to Tuskegee, sure I was focused on getting my degree, but I wanted to enjoy all the moments that came with being at Tuskegee, so when I graduated it didn't feel like I left anything on the table like I did at Poly.

The best area in which this jewel is applicable is meditation. The reason why I say that is because meditation gives you the opportunity to hit that pause button in your life and reflect on whatever is on your mind, heart, or spirit before you continue your journey. It can also be an opportunity to reflect on the moments you had in your life as well and ultimately give a peace of mind and a way to escape the stresses that life brings. In other words, give you a chance to be still and take a breath without getting lost in the challenges life brings.

So continue to strive toward your destination but never forget each moment you have as you travel toward your destination, because sometimes the enjoyment isn't always getting to the destination, it's the moments you have on the road toward your destination that may bring you enjoyment.

## How Did You Change Along Your Journey Vs. When You Began?

To piggyback off of reflection, the big question along your journey should be how you changed along your journey vs. how you began your journey. In other words, what did you learn about yourself as you went on your journey of life? This is where the importance of growth comes into play like I talked about earlier. As far as change is concerned, the moments I talked about appreciating and reflecting on allow you the opportunity of change. It allows you to evaluate what you need to do moving forward because the thing is if you are changing along your journey, you have to evaluate if the journey is even worth it. Muhammad Ali said it best, **"A man who views the world the same at 50 as he did at 20 has wasted 30 years of his life."** With that said, the older you get, your perspective of life should change. You aren't going to view the world the same way you did as a child when you're a teenager. You're not going to view the world in the same way as an adult as you will when you become an elder.

What I would encourage for you is to think about your journey and where you are now vs. five years ago or ten years ago. It could even be last week or yesterday. Ask yourself what has changed about me then vs. now. It could be physical, mental, or emotional. It could be maybe you have more confidence in yourself, or maybe you have become more committed to your mental health. The bottom line is as you go along your journey, I hope you slowly evolve into a better place in which you find fulfillment by the time the journey ends. People like to say, "It's not how you start, it's how you finish," but sometimes it is how you change along the way before you finish that should be considered, too. If you're finishing the same way you started, then it would have been better if you never started at all.

## Your Journey Is Unique; It Is Part of What Makes You Who You Are

The unique thing about life is that all of our journeys are unique. I think it's rare to find someone who goes on the same journey as you. Sure, you may have similar experiences, but for the most part I would say our journeys are different. The key is everyone has a journey, and everyone has a story to tell. I would also say your journey makes you who you are in the sense that it describes certain characteristics about you. Maybe your journey shows you're a fighter because you overcame so many challenges; maybe it shows you're a healer, or maybe it shows you're a visionary because you have manifested something wonderful to the world. Whatever it is, it makes you the person you are, and you should be proud of that. Never let anyone minimize your journey or put a time limit on it.

## We Don't Know Where the Journey Will Take Us, But That's What Makes It Special

What makes our journeys special is we never know where they will take us. The thing about life is it has its twists and turns, lefts and rights, and ups and downs. Sometimes when you travel down the road of your life, everything will be going great and then sometimes, you will hit a bump on the road. In some extreme cases, you might get knocked off the road. Trust me, I've been there both figuratively and literally, but you have to keep going because you never know where that road will take you. After all, **"life is a highway"** and yes, if you were a 90s kid who grew up in the 2000s, I got that from "Cars."

If we knew where the journey would take us, it wouldn't be as special. It would be like if someone told you how a movie or an episode of a TV show you hadn't seen before is going to end. Once it's ruined, it doesn't hit the same. When you think about life, it is like one big movie or TV show, and we're all playing our role to see how it will end. As Andre' 3000 said on one of my favorite songs from OutKast, "ATLiens," **"The world's a stage and everybody gots to play their part."** So we may not know where our journey will take us or what's in store for us, but if we keep moving forward, you'll be surprised where it takes us, and remember **"the journey of a thousand miles begins with one step"** as described by Lao Tsu.

# Notes and Insights

# CHAPTER 10

# THE GREATEST JEWEL OF ALL IS THAT YOU'RE A JEWEL

Now we have reached the final jewel in this book, which is to realize that the greatest jewel in your journey is that you're a jewel. Actually this is my favorite jewel because you have to have confidence in yourself if you're going to make it in this world. It starts with having a high self-esteem. When you don't have high self-esteem or confidence within yourself, it becomes a challenge to achieve the goals you want to accomplish on the path you want to create for yourself. It also is hard for others to take you seriously because, think about it, if you don't have confidence in yourself, how can others have confidence in you?

It goes back to when I was talking about manifestation. Once you manifest something, you have the confidence you can manifest what you desire, otherwise it will never happen. I think as we all navigate our journeys, there are probably periods or moments where we have lost confidence in ourselves because we forgot we were jewels. We probably had a period of low self-esteem and a lack of motivation. I've been there. Going back to high school, that's where I can say I first lost my confidence, and when that happened, I wasn't really motivated to do anything at the time. Once you lose confidence in yourself, it can be hard to get it back if you're not careful. When I lost confidence in myself, I didn't get it back overnight. It took time to work on myself to get it back. This isn't to say you won't have doubt because you're human. However, never let your doubt become a loss in confidence in yourself.

Losing confidence in yourself can lead to other problems such as self-hate or looking for constant attention and validation outside of yourself. For example, how often do we see people try to change their appearance because they don't like the way they look when the reality is they look fine just the way they are. Let's be real: we all do want some validation from other people, and there's nothing wrong with that. It just shouldn't be your sole source of validation. The thing that should matter is you have validation within yourself. It's great to get a moment in the spotlight, but the spotlight doesn't last forever. Other people are going to shine in the spotlight, and the question is whether you are going to be okay with that and be comfortable with the validation within you. You can tell when a person is comfortable with themselves when they don't always have the spotlight on them or can even be behind the scenes. Remember to never lose confidence in yourself and always know your worth. It goes a long way.

## Never Fall Victim to Imposter Syndrome

Speaking of loss of confidence, there's nothing worse than making your goal and thinking you don't belong there. That leads to imposter syndrome. Imposter syndrome is basically when you doubt your talent, skills, or accomplishments and have a fear you will be exposed as a fraud. It's basically the fact that you're stuck in your head and thinking the worst will happen. But the key is to never fall victim to it. When you have put the work into reaching your goal, you have to adopt the attitude you belong there. When you have imposter syndrome, you are placing a limit on your capabilities because you're in a state of doubt. I think everyone goes through imposter syndrome at some point. However, it's how you overcome it.

I think I experienced imposter syndrome when I first got my job coming out of graduate school. So, my job was to help the shipping team at the naval base I worked at with their printers and scanners to make sure they were operational to print their labels. I was also working on making sure they had the app to help them print their labels was working properly. Then, there was a maintenance contract that was needed to be created so that their printers could be fixed. We also had to get new printers so they would avoid having a work stoppage. Let's just say this was a huge responsibility I thought was going to be difficult to take on by myself. There were times I didn't want to make a mistake for a fear of doing something wrong. But the good news is I had a great team behind me to ensure they had the resources needed to fulfill their responsibilities, and over time these needs have been met. This doesn't mean things are always perfect, but with the team I work with behind me, I feel like I can confidently help the shipping team, whereas when I started I felt imposter syndrome.

Imposter syndrome may happen, but remember people say that the only real competition you have is yourself. Ultimately, it's up to you how you view yourself, and if you're a jewel then you should strive to be real. I think imposter syndrome can be solved by just coming out of your head. Be proud of the talents and accomplishments you have been blessed with and let them speak from themselves.

## Love Yourz

If there is any song that describes that the greatest jewel of all is that you're a jewel, it's "Love Yourz" by J. Cole off his album, "2014 Forest Hills Drive," which in my opinion is his best album so far. The line that stands out to me is when he said, "**No such thing as a life that's better**

**than yours.**" Now of course, people could have different interpretations about what this song means, but here is the lesson I got from the record: you should never compare your life to other people so much to the point where you end up hating your own, especially when you're comparing it based on status and material possessions.

Sometimes, we get so focused on where other people are in their life that we don't realize how good we have it in our life. For example, we think people who are successful are living stress free, living their best life, and are worry free. However, little do we know that these same people are hurting behind closed doors. Celebrities might be a perfect example. They have fame, money, status, and can pretty much get everything their hearts desire. But some celebrities suffer depression and other problems that the average person may not want to deal with. That's probably why J. Cole said that "**It's beauty in the struggle, ugliness in the success**" or "**For what's money without happiness or hard times without the people you love?**"

Another thing to know is sometimes we think our lives are so bad and unfilled that we fail to realize how great we actually have it, and there are people who may be doing worse than we are who ultimately wish they could be where we are. For example, you and your family may not live in the biggest house, but at least you and your family have a house. There are a lot of people who have become homeless wishing they could have a house. Or you may not live in a mansion, but you and your family live in a safe neighborhood, while sadly there are people who live in bad neighborhoods wishing they could find a way out to a better life. To quote J. Cole on this record, "**I grew up in the city and know sometimes we had less, compared to some of my ni**as down the block, man, we were blessed. And life can't be no fairytale, no once upon a time, But I be goddamned if a ni**a don't be tryin'.**"

Ultimately, I appreciate that the song tells you that your life is what matters the most and the flaws of seeking validation from other sources. You ultimately have to love yourself first before you can get others to love you. Also, you don't need material possessions to improve yourself. Don't get me wrong, we all like nice things, and there's nothing wrong with that. But when you're trying to validate yourself solely through material possessions, you're always going to be chasing validation. In other words, it's never enough. J. Cole said it best, **"To all my ni**as out there living in debt, cashing minimal checks, turn on the TV see a ni**a Rolex, and fantasize about a life with no stress, I mean this shit sincerely, and that's a ni**a who was once in your shoes, living with nothin' to lose, I hope one day you hear me, always gon' be a bigger house somewhere, but ni**a feel me, 'long as the people in that mother-f**ker love you dearly, ways gon' be a whip that's better than the one you got, always gon' be some clothes that's fresher than the one's you rock, Always gon' be a b*tch that's badder out there on the tours, but you ain't never gon' be happy 'til you love yours."**

And like there's no such thing as a life that's better than yours, the same should be about your journey. There's no journey that's better than yours, and that is why I say your jewels are in your journey. The keyword is your, and you should love it. If I tell you that your journey needs to be the same as another person, then it's not your journey because it's not unique for you. So to close this, love the life and the journey that you have made for yourself, or to summarize that in two words: **"love yourz."**

## Jewels are Meant to Shine Not to be Hidden in the Dark

When you think about the purpose of any jewel, it is for it to shine. It's what draws your interest to it. No one is attracted to a dull jewel. Now being that you're a jewel, your purpose should be the same. You can't be afraid to shine, stand out, or be your own person, even if people don't like that about you. You can't spend your whole life following the crowd, especially when you see the crowd is headed on the wrong path. For those of you who grew up in church, you may have sung "This little light of mine, I'm going to let it shine." Then again if you didn't go to church, I'm sure someone in your family who went to church probably sang it. However, it is true. You are supposed to shine your light. Even the Bible says you should let your light shine before men and compares that to how people don't light a candle and put it under a bushel but on a candlestick so it can give light. Now I'm not saying that from a religious perspective but more so on the fact that we are supposed to be willing to share our light among others.

Now, I'm not saying you do things just to be seen by men, but be comfortable being yourself around other people. An example of this may be if you're a smart person, you might make the mistake of trying to dumb yourself down to fit in with other people. Once you do that, you just hid your light under a bushel or you just became a jewel with no shine because you're not being authentic and people who actually know you for being smart are going to see through you.

I think when we're young we try to hide our light so we can fit in with others, but as we get older we start looking for our identity and get to the point where we're happy being who we really are. In other words, we get to the point where we take off the masks we have been using to hide who we really are. What I want you to realize is you have certain talents and abilities that can be shown in the world, and as a jewel I want to see you shine as bright as you can.

## Pressure Makes Diamonds

If you want to know how any jewel is made, it's going to require pressure. That means it is going to take some hardship. For example, a diamond starts off as a lump of coal, but through the process of pressure, it becomes a diamond. As humans, we're pretty much the same. No one goes through life without some form of hardship or pressure, but when we overcome that pressure or hardship, it makes us better people or a jewel. Some people like to use the phrase **"a diamond in the rough"** for people who have great potential and with some guidance could be great. Well, when you go through hardship, people might be able to see that you have potential to do great things, and if you're fortunate to get some guidance, you might become a jewel.

Speaking of pressure and hardships, I heard Chris Rock say that **"pressure makes diamonds, not hugs."** He said, **"hug a piece of coal and watch what you get, you get a dirty shirt."** Now the context of this was that he was speaking about bullies and how at his daughter's school they had a no bully policy during his Netflix special "Tambourine." He joked how because of this he wanted to take his daughter out of the school. He mentioned the fact that **"school is supposed to prepare you for life. Life has assholes, and you should learn how to deal with them as soon as possible. God forbid you wait till you're thirty to find out people ain't shit. That's a lesson you need quick."** Now the thing is, life does bring its bullies, but sometimes because of the hardships or pressure that it brings, life itself can be a bully. Remember, life is not fair, and I hope you didn't have to wait until you became thirty to figure that out. If you did, bless your heart. You just wasted thirty years of your life, my friend.

However, what matters is it's not that you were bullied, but how you overcame the bullying. There are a lot of successful people who went through hardship but never gave up and let life push them around. They just found a way to adapt and keep going. Sometimes we need a challenge, whether it's a person or a task to help us grow and become the person we want to be. This leads us back to Chris' point that pressure makes diamonds and not hugs. Now, hugs are nice, and I'm sure everyone likes them, but in certain situations hugs are not helpful. An example of life giving you pressure would be if you lose your job and all of a sudden cannot pay your rent, your landlord is still going to want their rent money. They are not going to let you give them a hug and say you can stop paying your rent for as long as you need to. You're going to have to overcome this hardship in order to have some way to have a place to stay.

I use myself in this next example. During all the drama that I was in while in high school, from failing in school, being in a cult, not having much of a future, my father put a lot of pressure on me. He never stopped loving me, but he gave me tough love. Now would I like to have had more moments of him not yelling or getting on me for being in a bad situation? Yes. Would I have liked for him to tell me that "you're doing the best you can do son." and give me a hug? It would have been nice, but that's not what I needed. I needed pressure and brutal honesty to get myself together. Honestly, because of all that pressure and tough love, it made me into the jewel I am today. Now, I'm in a place where I don't have to worry about all that yelling anymore because my father pushed me to be better than I was. Guess you can say, he saw me as that "diamond in the rough." And that's how life goes sometimes; you need some pressure to become a jewel, and hopefully when you become a jewel, you can get a good hug from somebody you love down the road.

## Once You Know You're a Jewel, Other Jewels in Your Journey Will Fall Into Place

The beauty of knowing that you're a jewel is all the other jewels I mentioned in this book so far can be accomplished and can be summarized by this last jewel. If you know you're a jewel, you'll never take life for granted, you'll learn from your mistakes, you'll have a great role model, and you'll appreciate the people who are always there for you. You're not going to let others put you in a box, realize the struggle can be a blessing, always give back and help others, know that positivity is good for the soul, and focus on the journey as opposed to the destination. I guess you could say that if you want to go far along your journey, it starts with knowing yourself and your worth.

When you think highly of yourself in a humble way, you start to move differently in life. You realize you won't be able to make the same decisions that you used to, and that shows growth and maturity. It pretty much boils down to knowing who you are. As the saying was in ancient Kemet (Egypt), **"Man (Woman) know thyself."** Ultimately, these are some benefits of knowing your jewel. Now when you forget you're a jewel, it is going to reflect in your life. It will show in your character and how you conduct your life. Think about it: how can you call yourself a jewel when you treat others disrespectfully, or you dress like a bum, or you're out here sagging your pants, or you don't take care of your mental or physical health, or if your life is in a constant state of chaos, and you make the same mistakes and never learn from them? Being a jewel is an attitude and a way of life. You can say you're a jewel, but you have to live it, too, and once you do, you'll be able to pick up on the other jewels you find along your journey, In the end, knowing you're a jewel makes the journey easier as opposed to not knowing you're a jewel and going through a more difficult path.

Finally, never forget to remind others that they're jewels, especially when they're going through the challenges of life. See everybody has a source of inspiration, and that source of inspiration may be you. The way I see it, if every person in the world realizes they are a jewel, it may motivate them to live their true potential. However, it starts with you. Before you can remind other people that they are jewels, you have to come to the realization that you're one first. As Michael Jackson said on "Man in the Mirror." **"If you wanna make the world a better place, take a look at yourself and then make a change."** It's all about taking pride in who you are and more importantly taking pride in who we are as a people. That's why I call myself a jewel, and I hope you'll do the same.

Finally, as a jewel, I want you to find what jewels inspire you, whether they be people or lessons. Make sure you apply them and share your inspiration with the world because everyone has a story to tell. I appreciate you reading about the jewels I have learned on my journey. I guess you can say we reached our destination as far as this journey is concerned, but never forget there are many jewels out there. You just have to look for them. Remember, seek and ye shall find. Just because we reached the end of this book doesn't mean your journey is over, because life is a marathon and not a sprint. As the late great Nipsey Hussle said, **"The marathon continues."** So share the knowledge and experience you have gained along your journey because if it can help others, it needs to be shared and, who knows, maybe you'll be inspired to write the jewels in your journey. I'd love to read about it. So, with that said, I wish you well along your journey, and I hope you find many jewels along the way. From one jewel to another, I wish you luck, peace, and blessings along the way. You got this!

# NOTES AND INSIGHTS

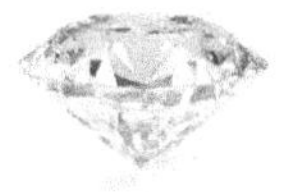

# ABOUT THE AUTHOR

I am Elijah Lewis. I am from Baltimore, MD, and I'm a graduate of Baltimore Polytechnic Institute, Tuskegee University, and Morgan State University. In addition to being an author, I am an engineer with NAVSEA in Indian Head, MD. Growing up, I know I was blessed with success, but definitely had my challenges and made my fair share of mistakes. However, my philosophy is that life is a journey, and along that journey, you can find a lot of jewels if you look hard enough. I also know the importance of helping others and that everyone has a story to tell. I went from being a person with a 2.58 GPA in high school who really didn't have the brightest future, to being an engineer and author due to the people who have helped me along the way.

I know what it's like to be lost on the journey of life. It can be a dark and lonely feeling, but with the right help you can get back on track. That's why I wrote "Your Jewels Are In Your Journey: Life Lessons to Lead You to Your Optimal Self." I believe everyone has the power to be their best potential, and that comes with experience as you go through life. My goal is to inspire readers to the point where they realize the power that they have within them, and like a jewel, realize the brightness they have. Ultimately, the vision I have is for my readers is to realize life is the biggest teacher, and if you pay attention, you can get great results.

I had never considered writing a book until I was asked by Matthew C. Horne of Lightning Fast Publishing Company, who I thank dearly for this opportunity. I felt it would be a great opportunity to write something impactful and share experiences with others that I've never shared before as a source of inspiration. At the end of the day, I'm just a guy that wants to see you win out here. For more information about me and my book, please visit www.yourjewelsareinyourjourney.com.